Leadership Bloopers and Blunders

How to Dodge Legal Minefields

Hope M. Jordan, Henry I. Willett, Jr.,
W. George Selig, and Andrea P. Beam

ROWMAN & LITTLEFIELD EDUCATION

A division of

ROWMAN & LITTLEFIELD PUBLISHERS, INC.
Lanham • New York • Toronto • Plymouth, UK

PUBLISHED BY ROWMAN & LITTLEFIELD EDUCATION

A division of Rowman & Littlefield Publishers, Inc.
A wholly owned subsidiary of The Rowman & Littlefield Publishing Group, Inc.
4501 Forbes Boulevard, Suite 200, Lanham, Maryland 20706
http://www.rowmaneducation.com

Estover Road,
Plymouth PL6 7PY,
United Kingdom

British Library Cataloguing in Publication Information Available

Library of Congress Cataloging-in-Publication Data

Leadership bloopers and blunders : how to dodge legal minefields / Hope M. Jordan ... [et al.].
p. cm.
Includes bibliographical references.
ISBN 978-1-60709-133-2 (cloth : alk. paper) — ISBN 978-1-60709-134-9 (pbk. : alk. paper) — ISBN 978-1-60709-135-6 (electronic)
1. School management and organization—United States—Case studies. 2. School administrators—Professional relationships—United States—Case studies. 3. School administrators—Legal status, laws, etc.—Case studies. 4. Educational leadership—United States—Case studies. 5. Actions and defenses—United States—Case studies.
I. Jordan, Hope M.
LB2805.L342 2010
371.2'011—dc22

2009031913

Printed in the United States of America

∞™ The paper used in this publication meets the minimum requirements of American National Standard for Information Sciences—Permanence of Paper for Printed Library Materials, ANSI/NISO Z39.48-1992.

Contents

Foreword

What a hoot! When I read *Leadership Bloopers and Blunders,* I laughed so hard I couldn't put the book down.

As you read these true stories about leadership blunders and misfortunes, and recall similar incidents in the news, a persistent inner voice says, "There, but for the grace of God, go I."

By collecting stories about true, yet bizarre incidents and raising questions about how leadership decisions are made, the authors put you on the scene as the proverbial fly on the wall. You are compelled to ask, "What would I have done differently in that situation? Will an incident like that be my own legacy? How can I avoid being thrust into the media spotlight - looking like a fool or worse?

The authors explain that "this book is intended to expand thinking, prepare leaders for the real world, encourage reflection and discussion, and possibly result in a little laughter as you read." We are fortunate. The authors accomplished their objective with their true stories and thought provoking questions. Laugh, reflect, enjoy, and learn from the experiences of others."

—Peter W. D. Wright, Esq.

Peter W. D. Wright, Attorney at Law is the Co-founder of Wrightslaw. He has an active schedule as an advocate, which includes his work as an author, speaker, and an adjunct faculty member of William & Mary School of Law (www.wrightslaw.com).

Preface

Have you ever worked in a place where the supervisor, principal, or boss did something that just made you wonder, "What in the world just happened?"

No matter where you work, in education, the business world, the private or public sector, there are always those leaders who act or speak before they think of the consequences. Unfortunately, this happens far too often in our schools.

Welcome to our book, *Leadership Bloopers and Blunders,* a "common sense" book on what ***not*** to do as a leader. The book is divided into six distinct chapters. Chapter 1 discusses the origin of the book, hence the title, *Leadership Bloopers and Blunders.* Chapters 2 and 3 will share "real-life" stories based-on actual events. Some stories are based-on actual court cases or events that made the news while others are compiled from events shared by colleagues. Chapter 4 highlights legal and good sense commentary from Dr. Willett on how to stay out of trouble and further investigates special education law. Chapter 5 discusses Dr. *Selig's 10 Leadership Principles* and positive leadership practices. Chapter 6 closes the book with final thoughts. Finally, the appendices offer resources to support leadership.

This book took shape as the authors, who have worked in various educational roles in both public schools and the private sector, recounted several stories. At first the stories were fun to share, but it was soon decided that these stories would be a great tool to help advance leadership skills.

Dr. Jordan's keen sense of observation and experiences in both K-12 and higher education led to the concept of this book. She compiled many of the stories from news reports, her personal experiences of over 30 years, and numerous conversations with teachers and leaders.

Dr. Willett was consulted for his brilliance and good-sense judgment on school law. He has presented to over 800 faculty and staff groups, spreading common sense to teachers and administrators as he notes the following issues that all too often can get administrators into "hot water":

- Improper physical contact—for example the male administrator who walks down the hall with his arm around female students.
- Sexual Harassment—for example an administrator who continued to lick his lips at a female teacher.
- Negligence—for example the administrator who saw two students posturing to fight and walked by (without a word) because school had not begun.
- Leaving students unattended—for example the administrator who sent a student out of the portable, in the winter weather, and forgot about him.
- Religion—for example the administrator who continues to lead athletic teams in prayer before a game.
- Dress code—for example the administrator who told a teacher she could see her crotch through her skort.
- Bullying—for example the administrator who says, "Boys will be boys."
- Corporal punishment—for example the administrator who assigns push-ups to students who run in the hall.
- Unnecessary force—for example the administrator who hits a student with a closed fist.
- Child abuse and neglect—for example the administrator who continually noticed a student with no winter coat on (in the winter) and observed that the student came to school in the same clothes each day.
- Stealing—for example the administrator who had a gambling addiction so he decided to "borrow" funds from the school. He actually got caught putting the money back!

Dr. Selig shares his 10 Leadership Principles to advance leadership skills by challenging leaders to lead with heart as well as mind. He has an outstanding ability to get to the heart of leadership, people.

As the youngest member of the team, Dr. Beam shared her experiences and reiterated the current situation in the schools by sharing her recent observations.

Several people deserve thanks for supporting this effort. First, we would like to thank our families for their on-going support and love. Dear Hannah Miltenberger, your work throughout the editing and formatting has been so appreciated. Kerry Baggaley, Rhiannon Jordan, and Gail Derrick: thank you for your professional input as we refined the topics and completed the editing. Thank you, all.

As you venture through this book, we would like each reader to ask, "Has this ever happened to me? Have I ever done this to anyone? Have I ever seen or heard about a similar situation?" If so, please join us as we scratch our heads and laugh our way through based-on true stories scenarios.

***The "based-on true" stories have characters who are fictional (except those related from actual court cases or newspaper accountings). Any resemblance to real people is purely coincidental.

Chapter 1

Introduction—Leadership Bloopers and Blunders

With over a century of experience between them in special education, education, leadership, and the law, Dr. Hope Jordan, Dr. Henry Willett, Dr. George Selig, and Dr Andrea Beam sometimes think they have seen it all. All they have to do is open the newspaper, and another story like the one reported by San Diego News in 2002, *Assistant Principal Demoted Over Thong Check* (10News.com) surprises them again. In fact, this book was nearly titled *No Thongs Allowed* based on that article! Ultimately, we settled with *Leadership Bloopers and Blunders* instead.

Leadership Bloopers and Blunders is a compilation of twenty based-on-true stories of leadership gone amuck that promises to shock and amaze even seasoned leaders. While most of the stories verge on absurdly funny, others just make one say, "What were they thinking?" and shake a confused head. At least one is downright macabre and some are just plain sad, but all are based-on-true stories.

Many of these stories are compiled from the authors' personal experiences. A few are classic cases that ended in court or hit the newspapers. Ultimately, each teaches a lesson. Some lessons are those of good sense and ethical judgment. Others are a lesson on the law. This book is for leaders in general, aspiring leaders, educational leaders, or those who study leadership.

It is the authors' intent to improve leadership by taking a hard look at what can go wrong when leaders seemingly lose their minds momentarily and make bad decisions. *Leadership Bloopers and Blunders* recounts based-on-true stories, asks thought provoking discussion questions, includes Dr. Henry Willett's expert response to these events, and concludes with Dr. George Selig's 10 Leadership Principles in an effort to suggest a better way to lead. The authors truly hope that readers will laugh, learn, question, and reflect as they read.

Welcome to *Leadership Bloopers and Blunders.* This book has been in development for over twenty years. As we struggled to choose a title, several options were reviewed. We overrode our first option, *Nipples and Crotches,* in an effort to be a little less offensive—although two of the stories below highlight the reason this title was considered. We also considered *No Thongs Allowed,* as mentioned above, but after consulting with the publisher we decided against that title, too.

The vocabulary we chose not to use in our first title options was used by leaders in stories that follow, so we would like to open with an apology for the offensive topics or terminology that comprise parts of this book. It is by no means our intent to offend. However, since the following stories are all based-on true stories, we will honestly share stories that include sensitive topics, issues, and vocabulary.

In the real world—the following topics are dealt with on a regular basis. We intentionally make light of some of these situations and use them in a manner that will allow others to grow and learn leadership lessons from less than optimal circumstances. Please accept our apology—in advance.

Although we ultimately chose *Leadership Bloopers and Blunders* as the title for this book, for quite some time we seriously considered naming it *Nipples and Crotches* or *No Thongs Allowed.* Every time we verbalized those initial titles we cringed, blushed, and pretty much nervously laughed out loud. This terminology was used in real leadership situations (as you will see in the stories that follow), but we didn't want to have people cringing and blushing (laughing is good) or misunderstanding the intent of the book. Our publisher preferred *Leadership Bloopers and Blunders,* so we chose the more socially acceptable title in an effort to offend fewer readers.

For those easily offended—we beg your forgiveness and encourage you to choose another book. For those with thicker skin, this book is intended to reflect the real world, expand thinking, prepare leaders for authentic situations, encourage reflection and discussion, and result in a little contemplative laughter as you read.

Without further adieux, we open with the three stories that influenced the ultimate title of this book, *I Find Your Nipples Disturbing, Is That Your Crotch I See?,* and *No Thongs Allowed.* Although all three of these opening stories verge on the issue of harassment, many other topics are addressed throughout the book, so please continue reading as we address several other topics in subsequent chapters. These first three stories, as others in the book, are based-on true stories. Names, places, and events have been changed to protect the guilty (or innocent - as all are innocent until proven guilty)!☺

I FIND YOUR NIPPLES DISTURBING

On any given day, school leaders may find a need to have a sensitive conversation with faculty or staff. Giving these conversations a few minutes of careful thought prior to having them is always a good idea. The leader in this story obviously did not think before speaking, as the following incident attests. The first time we heard this story, we were shocked. After we shared the content with a few colleagues, we were amazed to hear that several others had similar stories to share (their own or some they had heard). So—the story below is a compilation of a number of stories.

Our teacher— let's call her Ms. Oblivious—is an excellent teacher. She has several years of experience and is admired by her colleagues for her professional expertise, and is liked personally for her laid back personality. She is well-respected by parents, students, teachers, and administrators alike. She has never been called to the Principal's office for any reason other than to settle student issues (behavior, grading, parent concerns, etc). Well—at least not until today!

Ms. Oblivious was not the least concerned when Mr. Tactless (the principal) informally asked her to stop by his office after school. He had mentioned it briefly during lunch after they'd had a long conversation about her concern for a student's lack of progress in her reading class. She thought he wanted to discuss a new third grade pilot reading program she had been hearing so much about.

After school she had several tasks to complete before leaving for the weekend, and had frankly filed the principal's request in the back of her mind without much thought. By the time she was done with her work, most teachers had already made that typical hasty "Friday of a holiday weekend" retreat from the building.

She was surprised to see Mr. Tactless still in his office when she went to sign out for the weekend. He smiled, casually greeted her, and then said, "Do you have that minute now?" She said, "Sure," and followed him into his office. She was a bit concerned when he closed the door, as he normally left it open when he met with teachers.

Mr. Tactless obviously wanted to get on with his holiday weekend too, as he opened with, "Let me get right to the point. I find your nipples disturbing." Ms. Oblivious blushed and choked out, "Pardon me?" feeling immediately uncomfortable—especially since the office door was closed and they were alone. She then asked him what he was talking about.

He continued by clarifying, "I am sure that you may not be aware that your nipples are showing through your blouse. I understand that sometimes our rooms are a bit cool, which can cause this situation. My wife tells me there are bras with slight padding that control this situation?" Ms. Oblivious was speechless and just sat there. Mr. Tactless smiled and told her that he was sure she would correct the problem. He thanked her for stopping in and got up to open the door. Ms Oblivious mumbled, "You are welcome." and scurried to the ladies' room to assess the situation.

The bathroom temperature (or embarrassment) must have warmed Ms. Oblivious, as she did not see any problem at that time. She quietly went home and purchased extra padded bras over the weekend. She also started making sure that material (even in summer outfits) was a little more heavily textured in everything she wore to school. After all—one certainly does not want to go around disturbing others with their nipples.

Discussion:

1. Do you agree or disagree with how the situation was handled by school administration? Explain.
2. Could the teacher grieve the treatment? Why or why not?
3. How could the outcome be different?
4. Were there guidelines for the principal to follow, and did he do so?

IS THAT YOUR CROTCH I SEE?

Teachers should always dress in a professional manner. Individual taste, current fashion, school district dress code, and local norms are a few components that impact what any given teacher might choose to wear on any given day. This all influenced one professional's choice as she dressed for school her first month back following summer break.

As an experienced teacher, she did not put much extra thought into her outfit. She had seen professional women wearing the new skort suits throughout the summer. From her perspective, they were a perfect solution for female teachers, providing both comfort and style. She actually took exception to teachers wearing jeans and thought them unprofessional, even on casual days. Most often she dressed more formally. Even on school spirit day, she would choose nicer khaki type pants rather than the dressed-down jeans that others might wear.

She also felt that many teachers were too often overly casual—even sloppy—in their professional appearance. With all of that in mind, on most days she took extra effort to dress nicely, to wear stockings, matching shoes, and jewelry, and to choose dresses or skirts as her professional apparel. She also knew that what one wore to school was pretty much individual choice, often guided by very broad dress codes.

As she dressed for school, she was excited about starting a new year. The navy blue, skort suit was full, skirty, and feminine, yet professional. She was wearing a silk blouse, pantyhose, patent leather flats, and tasteful jewelry to finish off her professional look. The matching burgundy cuffs and belt added a little color to this tasteful outfit. Skorts by nature are comfortable and allow a teacher to move a bit more freely as they work with small children. So her new outfit added a lilt to her step as she left for school that day.

The outfit brought immediate compliments as she stopped at a convenience store for a soda on the way to work, and those compliments continued throughout the day. Most didn't realize that the outfit was a skort as it looked more like a skirt. Around mid-day as she walked down the hall, the principal walked toward her, smiled, and greeted her with a cheery, "How are you today?" All in all—it was a really good day and as she went home she did not give her outfit a second thought.

The next day, the same teacher who had chosen to wear a skort the day before was called to the office. She was wearing a dress (again with nice shoes, jewelry, etc). As she entered the main office, the principal was standing off to the side in the nurse's office doorway and motioned for the teacher to come in. The teacher entered, and the principal abruptly (while standing in the doorway between offices) began her conversation with, "Were you wearing shorts in school yesterday?"

The teacher was a bit confused, as the principal had seen her in the hall and greeted her the day before. The teacher responded, "No, I was not wearing shorts yesterday." The principal inquired further, "Were you wearing an outfit that was split up the middle?"

The terminology describing her apparel made the teacher very uncomfortable, and the fact that she was being angrily grilled in public aggravated that discomfort, but she answered, "I was wearing a lovely skort suit yesterday, and you saw me in the hall wearing it."

The principal continued angrily, "Don't ever wear shorts in my building again. I have been meaning to talk to you about how you dress." She then stretched out her arms to show a continuum and said, "On a scale of 1 (shaking her right hand) to 10 (shaking her left hand) your dress is generally down here (shaking the right hand again). You need to dress more professionally. Perhaps I can share some catalogues with you." She then smiled and said, "Don't do that again. I will talk to you later." and dismissed the teacher.

The teacher left the office in shock. As she walked down the hall close to tears she reviewed how she normally dressed (usually dresses or skirts and often complimented) with stockings and nice shoes, jewelry, etc. She passed the classroom of a very young teacher who was wearing a really cute white blouse and black skirt (the blouse was a little low cut in her estimation), and the classroom of an older lady who always wore tennis shoes, polyester pants and checked shirts (something the skorted teacher thought was too casual and more appropriate for a walk in the woods), and started asking herself if these teachers had received a tongue lashing about how they dressed, too.

Later that day, this same teacher reviewed the district dress code only to find that it was short and vague. It said something similar to the following: "Teachers are expected to dress in a professional manner that is appropriate." The teacher considered her outfit to be both appropriate and professional, and she left school that day even more confused by the conversation with her principal.

That evening the teacher received a call at home from her principal. This principal asked her to come to her office the next day, as she wanted to give her a copy of a letter of reprimand that was being put in the teacher's file. The letter was a detailed description of what the principal considered an inappropriate outfit that was "split up the middle in which the crotch is visible when she walks."

When the teacher asked her why she hadn't stopped her in the hall to discuss it when she saw her that day, the principal said she didn't remember seeing the outfit. As the long phone conversation went on, the principal revealed that the morning she had called the teacher to her office, she had just completed a conversation with another teacher who was wearing "shorts" in school and wanted to be sure that others didn't start wearing shorts. The skort teacher listened to the principal for nearly 1/2 hour as she went on about appropriate dress and the letter that would be formally filed.

At the end of the conversation, the skort teacher's husband tried to lighten the mood of the situation and asked (with a wicked smile), "What is her preoccupation with your crotch all about?" However, his humor was not appreciated at that point. That letter of reprimand loomed, and this teacher's crotch was now going to be mentioned in a formal letter and documented in her professional records. The entire situation was embarrassing.

A few days later, the other offending teacher approached the "skort" teacher to apologize. She had worn a skort outfit—more casual—that had grown tight over the summer, and she had not realized that her outfit did look more like shorts. When called to the principal's office she had mentioned the lovely skort suit worn by her colleague the day before, and was now mortified when she realized what trouble she had started.

This situation ended when the teacher ran into the Superintendent of Schools—wearing the offending skort suit—at a professional function. When she asked him how she looked, he was a bit baffled. After hearing the story, he asked that she send pictures of herself in the outfit downtown for formal review.

Being a bit camera shy (as evidenced by the look on her face in pictures), she was not happy about this situation. She even had to intentionally stand with legs apart in order for the split in the skort to show in the pictures, and she was mortified by the whole ordeal. In the end—the Superintendent did ask this principal to remove the letter from the file and to be careful about how she addressed her teachers' dress in light of a very broad dress code.

At the end of the year (children were not in the building), a colleague teased by yelling down the hall (as teachers were closing classrooms and wearing shorts), "Hey, -------------, is that your crotch I see?" The skort teacher responded, "Not my crotch. It must be someone else's crotch you see."

So—a very upsetting situation ended with a little humor and with the skort teacher requesting a voluntary transfer to another school. The next school year the principal did not heed the Superintendent's warning and started the year with a one-hour presentation on appropriate dress in her building. Thankfully—our skort teacher had moved on and decided to just let things go rather than pursue any legal options.

Obviously this administrator did not see error in her actions, as evidenced the following year when she expanded on her dress code with the teachers. The teachers worked through their teacher association, and the district responded by moving the principal out of the building to a downtown position. That move was initially seen as a reprimand, but resulted in future promotions a few years later.

Discussion:

1. Do you agree or disagree with how the situation was handled by school administration? Explain.
2. Could the teacher grieve the treatment and/or the formal letter of reprimand?
3. What other factors would you consider if you were part of the administrative team (i.e., school administration) hearing this incident for the first time?
4. How could the outcome be different?
5. Did the principal follow correct procedures?

NO THONGS ALLOWED!!!

On June 17, 2002, the San Diego News reported, "Assistant Principal Demoted Over Thong Check" (10News.com). This report caught the attention of educators and non-educators alike. Many were shocked and couldn't believe this situation could ever take place; some asked, "What was she thinking?" in reference to an assistant principal, who—according to students and the school security officer—performed an underwear check prior to a school dance.

Rita Wilson, assistant principal at a high school in California, was accused of lifting girls' skirts in an attempt to be sure that their "bottoms" were covered in case the girls should choose "freak dancing." She claimed that her motive was to be sure they did not expose themselves in public at the school dance.

Reports on the incident started surfacing in late April of 2002, shortly after a prom at Rancho Bernardo High School. Students told their parents that the vice-principal was asking girls with short skirts what kind of underwear they were wearing. If the girls said they were wearing thongs, skirts were lifted for the underwear check and/or the girls were asked to go home and change their underwear. Parents pointed out that there was nothing in the dress code prohibiting the wearing of thong underwear, and that an underwear check was not appropriate in any case.

Apparently, Wilson was motivated by an incident the prior year in which a girl exposed herself by lifting her skirt and removing underwear at a dance. Her defense was that she was trying to protect all and insure decency. During the investigation of this case, the assistant principal had many supporters who identified her as one who enforced rules and had good intentions. At one point she was put on leave during the investigation.

The entire incident was surrounded by controversy, with nine of fourteen speakers at the board hearing in support of the vice-principal. On the one hand, a well-intentioned vice-principal did a thong check before a school dance in an effort to enforce decency. On the other hand, girls reported feeling embarrassed and harassed by the situation, and a few even suggested that the vice-principal was a child abuser. Many parents were outraged at what they saw as an infringement of rights and an assistant principal acting inappropriately. In the end, this administrator was disciplined. We may never know what really happened.

Discussion:

1. Do you agree or disagree with how the situation was handled by school administration? Explain.
2. Do parents have the right to be outraged and/or to sue?

3. What other factors would you consider if you were this principal?
4. How could the outcome be different?
5. Did the principal follow correct procedures?

These three initial stories inspired the final title of this book. However, these examples are just the tip of the iceberg with regard to examples of leadership gone amuck. We hope that our introduction to *Leadership Bloopers and Blunders* has captured your interest. Keep reading—true stories are often stranger than fiction!

Chapter 2

Leadership Bloopers and Blunders: Good Judgment and Common Sense

TO SIGN OR NOT TO SIGN—THAT IS THE QUESTION

Ms. Dankasehr (Ms. D.) was completing her first year as an assistant principal at Parker Middle School and had called Mr. Inamazement (Mr. I.) to her office for his final evaluation. As Mr. I. entered the office, he politely greeted Ms. D. They had developed a good working relationship throughout the year and shared a professional respect for one another. Over the next 45 minutes, that respect was going to take a few twists and turns.

Ms. D. asked Mr. I. to take a seat as she held up what looked like his completed evaluation form and she stated, "This is the evaluation I completed for you last week after my final visit to your classroom." To his surprise, she tore that evaluation in half and dropped it in the garbage can sitting next to her desk. She then reached into her drawer and pulled out another evaluation form.

As he sat, still stunned, with his mouth hanging open and a furrowed brow, she stated, "This is the evaluation I have been told to give you." Still shocked and confused, Mr. I. just sat quietly looking at Ms. D. as she continued, "I would like you to understand that you have the right to ask any questions you like as we go over this evaluation. If at any time you have any questions about what I observed or what I have written here, you should ask your questions. If you ask questions, I will leave for a minute, get some guidance, and come back with an answer. Please be sure to ask questions and make your comments as we go. Do you understand?"

Although Mr. I. was somewhat confused, he was getting a sense that Ms. D. was not happy with the evaluation that she had been told to give him. She was giving him the opportunity to ask questions and make comments. In fact, she seemed to be encouraging questions and comments.

Mr. I. had noted as he read the first evaluation form (now lying face up in the bottom of the trash can next to the desk) that of the three possible levels of evaluation, US (Unsatisfactory), S (Satisfactory), and XE (Exceeds Expectations), he had initially been marked with XE most frequently and an occasional S, which indicated that he had done a pretty good job with his lesson. On the updated evaluation form that Ms. D was holding, with her final marks and comments, he had been marked with a few S responses and several US marks. This final evaluation reflected a less than satisfactory job overall.

As the evaluation process proceeded, Mr. I. made sure to stop Ms. D. whenever he was confused or disagreed with a level marked. He would then ask a question or make a statement. For example, when Ms. D commented on his lack of communication with parents, he quickly pointed out that he used the Homework Hotline, updated his class Web Page on a weekly basis when he sent home his weekly newsletter to the parents, and had several students on individualized notebooks with daily comments taken home to parents.

As he mentioned this, Ms. D. calmly smiled and said that she had noted these procedures. She wrote down some comments, excused herself for a moment, and left for a conference with the principal. She returned a few minutes later and apologized for the error and said that she would correct that on the final copy of his evaluation.

A few minutes later when a comment was made about his lack of accommodating individual student differences, he asked if she remembered the centers in his classroom and the portion of each lesson that addressed differentiated instruction. Again, Ms. D. smiled and said that she did remember, and excused herself for another short conference with the principal. As she returned, she again apologized and assured him that this would be corrected on the final evaluation copy. This went on for the remainder of the evaluation, with Ms. D. excusing herself a total of six times during the 45 minute session. Each time she left the room, Mr. I. glanced over at the torn evaluation form in plain view in the trash can.

At the conclusion of the conference, Ms. D. thanked Mr. I. for his time and asked if he thought they had made all of the necessary corrections on this evaluation to ensure that it was correct. He told her that he thought that they were on the right track. By this time, he had a sense that the principal had been trying to give him (for some reason) an evaluation that was lower than what he deserved, and realized Ms. D. was trying to help him. He was confused but stated, "Before I sign the final copy, I will make sure that we have it all corrected. If I do not feel that it is correct, I will be sure to make my own written comments directly on that evaluation." He smiled and left the office.

A bit dazed by all that had happened, he mentioned this strange situation to a colleague. That colleague commented, "I told you that our principal is not in favor of inclusive settings in this building, and you have been advocating a more inclusive program here. Do you think that she would rather have you transfer to another school?" Mr. I. left the building that day wondering if this were the case. While Mr. I. waited for his evaluation to be retyped, other teachers made similar comments.

Mr. I. and Ms. D never spoke of the incident again. The final evaluation form was corrected and signed by all. Mr. I. requested and was granted a transfer to another building that summer. Ms. D. resigned from the district and accepted a principal's position in a neighboring district that summer, too. We may never know what really happened.

Discussion

1. What do you think really happened?
2. Do you think MS. D. handled this situation ethically/legally? Explain.
3. Do you think Mr. I. should have taken the torn copy from the trash can and pursued further action? If so—why and what?
4. How might this situation have been handled differently?
5. Does an assistant principal always have to do as directed by a principal? Explain.

Further Discussion

What do ethics have to do with leadership? Are there certain character traits that good leaders should possess? This teacher was not given a fair and accurate evaluation. In essence, this assistant principal lied on the evaluation because she was told to do so by her principal. Sometimes a decision is complicated, as it may be legally correct but ethically wrong. Discuss ethics and positive character traits with regard to the role of both principal and assistant principal.

I LIKE YOU, SO. . . . I SAY 'YES'!

Before a student can qualify to receive special education services, a plethora of paperwork must be completed, meetings attended, and testing completed. Processes to qualify for special education are constantly being updated. Teachers and leaders have to remain current of all changes. For one rising ninth grade student, a rather interesting criterion was used to qualify for special services.

It began in August at the freshman open house for rising ninth graders. The assistant principal (AP) was greeting parents and students to welcome them to their new school. One mother (to protect her anonymity we will call her Mrs. X.) was memorable. Mrs. X. quickly approached the AP and was the epitome of graciousness. She began to explain how the middle school that her child attended did not follow through on necessary paperwork, and how she was worried that her daughter would not be getting essential services for the upcoming year.

Mrs. X. believed that her daughter was a student with a disability who was "falling through the cracks." The AP began asking a series of questions and found that the student was an honor roll student until she entered eighth grade. The mother reported that at that time, the student began experimenting with drugs and her grades quickly declined. Mrs. X. continued to share that she and her husband quickly pulled her daughter out of public school and sent her to boarding school with the intention of getting her back on track. Mrs. X. explained that they had decided to try public schools again and give her daughter a fresh start in high school.

The AP told Mrs. X. that it did not sound as though her daughter had a disability, but instead sounded like the drug involvement contributed to her decline in school. She continued to explain that qualification for special services was a team decision and that her daughter would be put on the next agenda.

After reviewing the student's cumulative records and reports from former teachers, the team decided that the student would not qualify for services. In spite of this, the meeting was held and Mrs. X. explained why she believed her daughter was a student with a disability. Feeling this case was clear-cut and that the student did not have a disability, the AP did not attend the meeting and had the department chair attend as designee.

In an interesting turn of events, the student was qualified under the Other Health Impairment (OHI) label because Mrs. X. was just so darned nice! The team suffered from a moment of "I like you, so I say yes!" The AP regretted not attending the meeting but decided to let it slide because she, too, wanted to help Mrs. X.

The student's first year in high school was pretty uneventful. Her Individualized Education Plan (IEP) was followed and monitored frequently. Mrs. X.

attended all meetings and was very helpful throughout the year. The next year was nothing like the first!

The student had slipped back into her old habits and began using drugs again. During her second year in high school she came to school for after-school tutoring and appeared "high" to the teacher. When questioned, the student replied, "Yeah, I went home to get high before coming back."

The first-year teacher quickly sent the student to the main office. The AP on duty was called to investigate and found marijuana residue in a small baggie inside the student's book bag. Protocol was followed, and Mrs. X. was immediately called to the main office to retrieve her daughter.

According to school guidelines, marijuana (or any other drug) use or possession (including residue) is a recommendation for a manifestation hearing and possible expulsion. In what seemed to be only a few minutes, Mr. X. (Dad) came storming down the hallway in a huff! He was not happy and was very combative. The principal decided to intervene and reduce the recommendation to a three-day suspension, because they all really liked Mrs. X.

Months went by without incident. The second incident occurred after school as the student was going to band practice. She decided to get a little creative this time, and actually made a pipe out of her instrument mouthpiece. She was caught, again, by her teacher who noticed her abnormal behavior and glassy eyes. Once again, the student was sent to the office and dealt with by the AP on duty.

Again, Mr. X. hastily stormed to the AP's office to retrieve his daughter. This time the school resource officer (SRO) was waiting. The administrator had been caught unprepared for Mr. X.'s aggressive behavior during the first incident, and this time they wanted to make sure the SRO was available in case of another incident.

After yelling at the AP and demanding to get the SRO's badge number (because Mr. X. accused him of planting the marijuana on his daughter), he took his daughter and rushed out of the office. Once again, the AP recommended a manifestation hearing and possible expulsion, but it was reduced to out-of-school suspension by the principal because they really, really liked Mrs. X.

The third, and final, incident happened near the end of the student's sophomore year. Her teacher brought her to the main office when she appeared to be "under the influence." A further investigation revealed that she was under the influence and had a baggie full of marijuana in her possession. This time, the original AP (the one who met Mrs. X. at the open house) handled the incident. She again recommended expulsion following the manifestation hearing, but this time, the recommendation was honored. The student was sent home with her father, the aggressive Mr. X!

Surprisingly, when the case went to Student Leadership it was decided to send the student back to school. She returned to finish off her year, but this time, numerous IEP meetings were requested by the parents and their new counterpart, the advocate (Mrs. A). It appears that Mrs. A. did not believe that the IEP and modifications from the previous year were ever followed correctly, and she was going to make sure everyone knew how "incompetent" they were when it came to dealing with this student!

Many meetings transpired for the remainder of the year, and there was daily contact (sometimes more than once per day) with the parents, Mrs. A., and school personnel. What began as a very friendly relationship was now contentious.

It seemed as though Mrs. A. continued to try to ruin the relationship between the school and the parents. The school repeatedly tried to rebuild the relationship, but they did not prevail. The case went to due process and was drawn out for months. School personnel felt the family and Mrs. A. told several lies under oath. This turn of events left the school parties feeling confused. The original AP and the department chair who sat in as designee continued to wonder if any of this would have happened had the school simply followed policy (i.e., not qualifying one for services because they liked the Mom), instead of following their hearts.

Discussion

1. Have you ever encountered a situation in which a particular student was qualified for special education services under false pretenses? Explain.
2. Could this situation have been handled differently? Explain.
3. Why did the parents secure an advocate after the first year? How should schools deal with advocates?
4. What can be done to maintain positive rapport with parents?
5. Could the AP, who did not attend the initial eligibility meeting, have called another meeting to reconvene and retract the disability status of the student?

Further Discussion

Was this really an ethical situation or does it cross the border into a legal situation? When should the law be involved regarding drugs and drug paraphernalia on school property? Did administration, by their actions, condone drug use? Discuss that fine line between ethics and legality that leaders must maneuver.

GOOD OLD-FASHIONED DISCIPLINE

There are times when one wonders if a return to the "good old days" might be a good idea. How many times do we hear parents and teachers lament how times have changed? Maybe we should go back to some of the old fashioned discipline techniques?

Mr. Star was considered a pretty darn good principal. He had grown up in the village of Countryside, had gone to school in the community, and graduated with a football scholarship after a winning year as a quarterback on the local football team. His ties to the school, parents, and students sometimes made his job more difficult, but most often were a benefit to him as a leader. He was not the strongest instructional leader, but he knew his strengths and weaknesses and had teamed up with a great assistant principal who led the instructional activities at Countryside High.

Mr. Star had the respect of the parents with regard to discipline. Most students knew that ending up in the principal's office for discipline was not a good idea, as Mr. Star was fair but tough. Old fashioned discipline techniques were often employed, and most of the community supported Mr. Star's approach.

Ms. Frankly was a single mother new to the community. As a working mom, she had a very busy schedule, but she was dedicated to her only son's education and knew that he needed to work hard to get into a good college. She visited Countryside High at least once a week just to stay in touch with what was going on at school.

She entered the building one Friday afternoon expecting to pick up her son after football practice. As she walked toward the gymnasium, she was surprised to see him sitting on the floor in front of his locker with a toothbrush in his hand.

He sheepishly looked up and said, "Hi, Mom. You are a little early. Give me a minute, I have to check in with Mr. Star and get my books." Ms. Frankly walked next to her son and asked, "Why were you sitting on the floor with a toothbrush?" The young man blushed and replied, "I wrote a message to one of my friends in marker on the side of the desk in Algebra class today. After I finished cleaning the desk, Mr. Star suggested that I clean my locker, too."

Ms. Frankly was very upset that her son was being reprimanded by having to clean the desk and the locker with a toothbrush. She felt that the embarrassment would do psychological harm to her boy and she said that she would have a talk with the principal. As she headed to the office, her son followed behind begging her to stay out of it, and said that he and Mr. Star had worked it out. Would you like to know what happened when she got to the office?

Discussion

1. Should a principal have students clean lockers with a toothbrush as a discipline technique? What are some other options?
2. How do you think this situation ended?
3. How should Ms. Frankly handle the situation?
4. What are a mom's rights?
5. What are the students' rights?

SAY WHAT YOU MEAN, AND MEAN WHAT YOU SAY

As an administrator or teacher leader, have you ever been to a school and realized that there's *one* teacher who seems to be doing it all wrong? You quickly decide that you're going to try to mentor this teacher, but everything you say falls on deaf ears? If you have been in this situation, you realize that you must take action into your own hands and put the teacher on an action plan.

Upon further investigation, you find that all their past evaluations are glowing! This is an awkward position. There's nothing worse than having to be "the bad guy" when there has been a history with a particular employee, be it a teacher, teacher's assistant, custodian, etc.

This excerpt is about leaders doing the right thing—"Say what you mean and mean what you say." This situation occurred recently in any school near you. The assistant principal (AP) was new to the building and just getting a "feel" for the staff and community. The principal called her into his office and said, "I want you to take care of teacher G."

The AP wondered what the principal meant by "take care of" and felt as though she were a character in a movie about the mob. As it turned out, the principal expected the AP to put teacher G. on an action plan. The teacher was still in her probationary period with the school system and was doing a bad job, so he wanted the AP to write her up and get rid of her before her probationary period expired. The AP liked to follow the rule of law, and she felt that his request was out of order. She appealed to him and assured him that if he gave her some time, she would mentor teacher G. so that she could meet his and the school system's expectations.

The AP worked diligently with teacher G. about once a month, to make sure she understood her requirements as a special education teacher. The AP pounded the law into teacher G., because this is where teacher G. seemed weak. Teacher G. did things her own way, in her own time, without much regard to the federal guidelines, state regulations, and district expectations.

Despite all the mentoring, the next school year teacher G. had made little to no improvement. Her rapport with the students and parents left much to be desired. The AP again conferred with and mentored teacher G. until all avenues had been exhausted.

The recommendations/requests by the AP were not being followed and the school was at a point of potential litigation if things continued. The AP consulted teacher G. and informed her that she would be placed on an action plan. Teacher G. was appalled! Never had *anyone* had a problem with her work habits or rapport, so she said. She was correct. Nothing had been documented, and there was no paper trail to provide evidence of the trouble.

When the AP went into teacher G.'s records, she was astonished! *All* of her evaluations from the last three years were superb!! How in the world could this have happened? Since the principal approached the AP over a year ago stating the problem, why were teacher G.'s evaluations flawless?

This situation happens far too often in our schools. Leaders have a duty to take care of business, mentor those who need mentoring, and handle those who are not doing a good job. In this particular situation, it took another year of constant documentation, several visits and observations from central personnel leaders, and many, many headaches to record the problem in order to take action with this teacher. Leaders need to be honest with their subordinates and explain and document their strengths and weaknesses.

Discussion

1. What should the AP have done from the onset after the principal initially requested that the AP "take care" of teacher G.?
2. How can leaders ensure that lax staff issues are addressed immediately?
3. Did the AP challenge her principal by not following his directions? Explain.
4. What would be an appropriate action for this situation?
5. From Teacher G.'s perspective, do you think that teacher G.'s work ethic should remain the same based on her previous evaluations because the new AP may simply be over-reacting? Might she feel, "Why was my performance good yesterday but not today?" Explain.

Further Discussion

This situation again can be addressed under good sense and ethics. How should leaders use teacher evaluations? Under most circumstances, should they be used to discipline or to instruct? What might schools do to cultivate a culture of excellence and ongoing professional growth? Discuss the issue of the use of teacher evaluations.

ENOUGH IS ENOUGH!

New administrators have enough on their plates with the new responsibilities of helping run a school, dealing with students, parents, and teachers, and following different rules with a different principal. As a result, it is imperative for them to watch and learn when coming into a novel environment. Leadership books stress the importance of observation as "the new guy" instead of coming in with a "change all" attitude in the first week. Unfortunately, one particular new leader did not read those leadership books.

A new assistant principal started at her very first school full of ideas and energy. She was going to make a difference and make her principal proud! She thought she was doing everything right. She was telling those teachers how things were going to be, and they were not going to get one over on her just because she was new! She was also going to let those parents know who was in charge, and she was going to let those students know the rules *right up front!*

During her first week in school, everything was going smoothly. She decided she was going to make a presence by being visible in the hallways between class changes. "Uh-oh," she thought, "I've forgotten my referral forms." She rushed back to her office to grab a stack of referrals for her hall duty. After all, one never knows when those pesky kids are going to act up and need to be taught a lesson!

She rushed down the hallway, referrals in hand, and caught two students lip-locked. "You can't display public affection in the middle of the hallway! Save that for after school hours!" she yelled. She hurried to get their names and wrote up her first referral. "I'm doing a great job," she thought.

She continued down the hall and found a group of boys wearing hats. "You can't wear headgear during the school day," she reminded them—but not before she had gathered all of their names to write referrals for them.

These actions continue for about a week or so until the "bright eyed, bushy tailed" administrator was called into the principal's office for a serious talk.

Discussion

1. What do you think the principal is going to say to the new administrator?
2. How do you think the students will respond to this type of action?
3. Do you think the assistant principal was correct in her actions? Explain.
4. How could the situation have been handled differently?

5. As a first year administrator, what are key ideas that you will keep in mind as you are making a "presence" in the hallways and leading by walking around?

Further Discussion

Students are not the only bullies. Was this assistant principal a bully? As leaders, how do we handle adults who bully students?

Chapter 3

More Leadership Bloopers and Blunders: Avoid Litigation through the Practice of Preventive Law

DIVISION OF CHURCH AND STATE

Amy was an excellent student who was doing exceptionally well in her eighth-grade Spanish class. She loved to travel with her parents and really liked the idea of speaking a foreign language. Cultures and geography fascinated her, and she worked hard to excel in class and get good grades.

Her Spanish teacher, Ms. Alondra, was enthusiastic about teaching Spanish, and designed creative assignments that kept her students interested in class. Ms. Alondra allowed the students to choose their own poster topic and design. The assignment was to design a poster in Spanish with English translation that would advertise a concept or character trait they felt was needed to better the world. She wanted them to think of things that crossed cultures like "courage" or "kindness."

As was characteristic for Amy, she took her assignment seriously, gave it a great deal of thought, and diligently worked to complete her assignment on time. Ms. Alondra was very pleased with the results of the entire class. She was so pleased that she got permission to display their work on one of the eighth-grade halls the next week. Two students stayed after school with Amy on Thursday to help Ms. Alondra hang the student work in the hall. The posters were colorful and creative.

The students were proud of their work, and since Spanish was translated to English on each poster, everyone who walked down the hall could enjoy the meaning of the posters while being introduced to Spanish vocabulary. Integrity, honesty, diligence, and love were a few examples of the advertisements proudly displayed in student work on the walls, and Ms. Alondra displayed the work of the entire class.

As Amy entered the building first thing on Friday morning, she was excited to see that the display already had student attention, and several teachers were also commenting on the quality of the work. Throughout the day as they passed their own creations, the Spanish students would glance at the work with proud smiles. At the end of the day, a puzzled Amy went to find Ms. Alondra to ask her a question. Amy's poster was no longer displayed on the wall, and she did not understand why there was an obvious spot of open wall where her poster had been carefully hung the prior afternoon. Ms. Alondra seemed uncomfortable as she quietly explained that the principal had asked her to remove Amy's work.

Amy was overtly upset as she asked why her poster was the only one taken down. Her Spanish teacher went on to explain that the principal felt that Amy's poster had "crossed the division of church and state line." Her teacher said that she had no choice, as the principal was very clear that she was not happy with the teacher and wanted the poster removed immediately.

Amy knew that some disagreed with her faith perspective, but felt that her poster, which simply read, "Jesus is love in any language!" was what she believed, and that she had as much right to discuss love as other students had to discuss the character traits that they had displayed. She felt she was singled out and walked to the office to talk to the principal. The principal chatted with Amy in her office and told her that some would find her poster offensive and that she wanted Amy to make another poster.

Amy left school that day feeling very uncomfortable and was not sure what to do. Her parents suggested that she do as the principal wanted and just not make a big deal of the situation. However, Amy determined that she had followed directions and had done a good job. She decided to ask more questions, and started by making (against her parents guidance and totally on her own) a phone call to the superintendent's office explaining the situation.

Amy was surprised when she was called out of class late on Monday afternoon. As she walked to the principal's office, she noted that her poster had been hung back up on the wall. As she entered the principal's office, the principal looked unhappy. She asked Amy to take a seat and asked her if she had called the Superintendent of Schools. Amy admitted that she had, as she quietly sat down.

The principal asked if Amy had noticed that her poster had been returned to the wall and Amy nodded her head. The principal said that she hoped since the poster was back up that she wouldn't be hearing any more about the situation. Amy said that she was happy to see her poster up with all the other students' work and felt like there was not anything else to say. The principal told her she could go back to class. Amy thanked the principal and returned to class.

Ms. Alondra said that she didn't know what had happened, but that she had been asked to put the poster back on the wall (with no further explanation) at her break that morning. Amy was just pleased to see that her work was back on display with the rest of the class, and that was the end of the story.

Discussion

1. Was the line between church and state crossed when Amy's poster was put on the wall with the rest of the class work?
2. Should the poster have been taken off the wall? Explain
3. Why do you think the poster was put back on the wall?
4. Should it have been put back up on the wall? Explain
5. How might you have handled a similar situation?

Further Discussion

Discuss the First Amendment and how this applies to student freedom of expression. Discuss the difference between teacher initiated and student initiated religious expression. When might it be appropriate to discuss religion in schools?

LOSING IT

Working in schools can be stressful. Whether one is in the position of leader, teacher, coach, or administrative support personnel, there are inherent stresses in any school setting. Constant interaction with students, parents, and colleagues, combined with high-stakes assessment and paperwork results in intense levels of stress that are difficult to deal with professionally. Following is one example of what might happen when adults lose it.

Mr. Friendly was an unassuming teacher who seemed to be liked overall by the students. He enjoyed the students and had been teaching for nearly ten years. He was not really passionate about his job, and his lack of excitement was reflected in lessons that were appropriate and included all the required components, but did not really result in students who were excited about literature and writing assignments. Basically, he had been teaching for ten uneventful years.

The teacher's lounge is often the place where teachers choose to share successes and vent frustrations. The teachers at P.T. Usual High where Mr. Friendly taught were like many others, but they noticed that Mr. Friendly seldom participated in any of the professional discussions. So—when Mr. Friendly started opening up and seemed to be a bit agitated by the behavior of some of his students, they paid attention to what he had to say. One colleague even suggested that Mr. Friendly let the assistant principal in charge of the discipline for his classes know what was going on.

Mr. Friendly took that advice and made an appointment to discuss student behavior with his assistant principal, Mr. Guy Strong. During their meeting, Mr. Strong thanked Mr. Friendly for the good job he had been doing. Mr. Friendly never sent students to the office, and Mr. Strong appreciated the fact that he did not have to deal with any problems from Mr. Friendly's students. The conversation ended with Mr. Friendly quietly leaving the office having glossed over how really upset he was with the students' behaviors.

The entire situation took a distinct turn for the worse the next day. Mr. Friendly had lunch room duty and was monitoring the lunch line when he asked a student to stop pushing in the line. The student was from one of Mr. Friendly's classes, and he turned and called Mr. Friendly a wimp. Mr. Friendly touched the young man's arm and asked him to step out of the line. The student turned rapidly and spit on Mr. Friendly as he yelled obscenities.

At this point, Mr. Friendly did not stop and think—he reacted. He quickly turned and punched the student. The student fell to the ground as Mr. Friendly turned and walked away. As the student got to his feet, he was yelling and asked for the police to be called as he shouted about being attacked by Mr. Friendly.

Mr. Friendly was arrested and charged with assault and battery for hitting a student. He was convicted and decided not to appeal the conviction. The sentence was six months in jail and a $2500 fine.

Discussion

1. How might the leader in this story, Mr. Strong, have unintentionally aggravated this situation?
2. How do you think this situation ended? Can you find any examples of similar stories in the news?
3. How might Mr. Friendly have handled the situation differently?
4. Do schools or districts have supports in place to help teachers who have having trouble dealing with anger or stress?
5. The teachers in the lounge suggested Mr. Friendly talk to Mr. Strong. Is there anything else they might have done to help in advance of this fight?

Further Discussion

Teaching and leading can be very stressful. How might co-workers and leaders better support good health and stress reduction? Have you heard of any school systems or businesses that are doing a good job in supporting better physical and mental health? If you work for Google, you are blessed with some benefits that people seldom find when they go work. Go to http://www.google.com/support/jobs/bin/static.py?page=benefits.html to read about what benefits Google offers its employees. What might we learn from Google that would lead to better education for both our students and our teachers? How might we do a better job in our schools?

CAUGHT WITH MY HAND IN THE COOKIE JAR

Principals work so hard to earn their position. Years of teaching lead into more years of being an assistant principal, and sometimes a year or so of being an administrative intern *before* becoming a "full-fledged" assistant principal. However, finally that glorious day comes, and the superintendant makes a phone call and asks, "Are you sure you know what you're getting into?" You can almost hear the angels sing, can't you?

For one ambitious principal, this was the case. He was a newly appointed principal and he was on the fast road to success. His reputation was increasing; he was young and motivated. He was what one would describe as a "go-getter" or a "mover and a shaker." Unfortunately, he also had a concealed gambling problem. For privacy purposes, we'll call this principal Dr. B.

Dr. B. would often go to Atlantic City or Las Vegas and amuse himself at one of the tables for hours. We all know the saying, "you win some, and you lose some." For this principal, losing was not an option. He remained at the tables to win his money back. Slowly but surely, his money was transferred from his pocket to the dealer's bank.

Dr. B. thought desperately, "Okay, I'll just 'borrow' a little more money from my savings account." But soon all of his money was gone and he even began dipping into his own children's college funds. At this point, he thought, "I have to leave!" and he headed home empty handed.

A few weeks later, however, the principal got a great idea. "I'll just borrow money from my administrative accounts. We aren't going to use that money any time soon; nobody will miss it." So he borrowed money from one of his "movable" accounts. His goal was to win back the money that he had lost and then some; that way he could return the money to the school.

Off to "Sin City" again, he went. "DING-DING-DING-DING—WE HAVE A WINNER!!!" Dr. B. had won!!! On this trip after only a few hours at the tables, the principal hit it big! He was able to put the money back into his personal accounts, and increase his kids' college funds. Additionally, Dr. B. had the money to return to school before anyone would even notice; life was good.

As the school week dawned, Dr. B. hurried to the school safe to return the borrowed funds. Little did he know that the bookkeeper was standing right behind him. The bookkeeper had grown suspicious when the books had not balanced over the last few weeks. Dr. B. was caught with his "hand in the cookie jar" while attempting to return the money! He was immediately removed from the school system. Rumor has it that he is dealing Black Jack in Atlantic City.

Discussion

1. As an aspiring principal, what was the mistake made in this scenario?
2. Were the consequences of his actions appropriate? Explain.
3. If you were an assistant principal walking into this situation (instead of the bookkeeper), would you have handled this situation differently? Explain.
4. What would be a good reason (i.e., one that would not warrant someone losing his/her job) to borrow school funds?
5. What amount of money could be borrowed without putting the principal at risk of losing his job? Explain.

Further Discussion

Discuss co-mingling—what does this term mean? Was this an issue of co-mingling or of outright stealing?

CYBER BULLY—ANTI-SEMITIC CYBER-BULLYING

Technology is a fabulous tool and can be used to advance our students' education in modern classrooms. That fabulous tool can also be used inappropriately and become very destructive. School leaders, teachers, parents, and students all need to be aware of the positive and negative uses of technology so that we are sure to monitor use and teach students how to use this tool appropriately—as we can see from our next story.

Landon was adjusting to his first semester in high school. He had his schedule down and had adjusted to getting up early to catch the bus at 6:30. He was making friends and liked most of his teachers (though he did think much of the work was boring). Overall, things were going well for this new freshman, so Landon's father was disturbed when he noticed that Landon was especially quiet at dinner several nights in a row.

Dad also noted that Landon seemed to be hiding the computer screen while he was working on his homework. When Dad questioned Landon, the young man stated, "I'm fine Dad. Nothing's wrong."

But—Landon's father was concerned, so after Landon went to bed he checked the computer history and found that Landon had been on some social utility sites and had been spending a great deal of time emailing and instant messaging a large number of friends and acquaintances. The next evening when Landon went to do his homework, Dad sat reading in the same room.

He noted when Landon started an email conversation and did not recognize the name of the person Landon was chatting with at the time. Landon also seemed irritated with his father's questioning, so Dad insisted. Landon lost his temper, screaming, "Dad, I can handle these guys, okay." At that point, Dad and Landon started a very serious conversation.

The serious conversation led Dad to some very revealing information. It seemed that Landon, who was Jewish, had been receiving a series of emails from a group of young people he had just met at his new high school. One young man, Jason, was sending him "Jewish Jokes" and was making anti-Semitic comments.

Although Landon said it was okay and that he could handle it, it was obvious that this was upsetting him. He did not seem as excited about going to school as he had been, and he was spending time responding to ugly email instead of working on homework. Landon and his father had a discussion about the situation. Dad talked to Landon about several important issues including anti-Semitism, respect for others' beliefs, politically correct statements, freedom of speech, and the correct use of the Internet. After a long discussion, Landon agreed that Dad should talk to the school principal about the situation.

The next day, Dad made an appointment and had a conversation with Landon's principal. Although the principal seemed sympathetic and supportive, he stated that he could not release any information about the offending student; and since this incident happened at home, he didn't feel the school had jurisdiction in this case.

Dad left the office rather frustrated, but bumped into the school counselor on his way out. She listened and suggested that although she couldn't release any information about the other student, she could call the other parents and make them aware of the situation. She asked Landon's father if she could give them his name and phone number if they asked for it, and he agreed.

That night, Landon's father got a phone call from Jason's parents (who were very embarrassed and apologetic). The two families ended up meeting and working out the situation. How might this story have ended differently if Dad had not bumped into the school counselor on his way out of the school?

Discussion

1. Discuss issues modern schools face with technology and topics like cyber-bullying.
2. What responsibility and authority do schools have in situations that have to do with their students but happen at home?
3. How might this principal have handled the situation differently?
4. Do teachers, leaders, or counselors have opportunities to address sensitive topics like anti-Semitism? Should they? If so—how?
5. What stories that have recently been in the news highlight the dangerous nature of cyber-bullying?

Further Discussion

Dr. Phil McGraw recently discussed the topic of cyber-bullying on the Dr. Phil Show. Some research done by Jay McGraw suggests that parents and teachers do not have any idea how prevalent and dangerous cyber-bullying has become. Discuss what schools might do to lead the way in terms of educating teachers, parents, and students about cyber-bullying.

HEY, THAT'S NOT MY "JOHN HANCOCK"!

An experienced assistant principal decided at the end of his fourth year that paperwork had become overwhelming. Administrators are to observe "seasoned" teachers at least once every other year. In this particular case, the administrator became more comfortable with his position than he should have, and decided to observe certain teachers and to sign off on their final evaluation, as well.

The situation escalated as a teacher was gathering information to submit for a Career Teacher application. She went to the head secretary at the school and asked for her last three years of evaluations to attach in her portfolio. The secretary provided the paperwork. The teacher noticed that the latest evaluation contained her name signed by someone else. "Hey, that's not my John Hancock!" fussed the teacher. When the principal discussed the incident with the teacher and the assistant principal, the assistant principal replied, "I wasn't marking her down; as a matter of fact, her scores were higher for her final evaluation."

The administrator did not see error in his actions because the teacher signed her previous evaluation, so why wouldn't she sign the final evaluation which contained higher marks? Unfortunately, school administration did find fault with this and actually demoted the assistant principal back to the classroom.

Discussion

1. Do you agree or disagree with how the situation was handled by school administration? Explain.
2. Could the administrator grieve the action of being sent back to the classroom for his first "mistake?"
3. What other factors would you consider if you were part of the administrative team (i.e., school administration) hearing this incident for the first time?
4. How could the outcome be different if the teacher went directly to the assistant principal for her evaluations instead of going to the head secretary?
5. Did the principal follow correct procedure?

Further Discussion

Do we have a case of forgery here? Discuss the topic of forgery.

BEAUTY AND THE BEAST

Nicole was excited as she rode the bus home from school. She was going to be participating in a Miss Teen Pageant in just over a week. She was really nervous about the competition, as she was a little bit shy, and competing in front of an audience was frightening.

Her modeling classes were preparing her to walk in the evening gown competition, and she had been practicing her violin for the talent competition. She was too embarrassed to tell her friends about the competition.

As Nicole turned thirteen, she seemed to become more quiet and sensitive about her height (she was the tallest girl in her classes). Her mother had suggested the modeling classes as a way to boost her confidence and poise. The modeling school instructor had been the one to encourage Nicole to participate in the teen pageant.

Nicole was excited about her approaching pageant as she sat with her little brother in the back of the bus while they rode home from school. She noticed a group of kids from their neighborhood huddled and whispering in seats closer to the front of the bus. They were pointing at the siblings and laughing. Both Nicole and her brother ignored them, as they knew they were a group of neighborhood bullies.

When the bus came to a stop at the end of their block, Nicole and her brother exited the bus. The group of bullies was standing at the bottom of the bus stairs, and as Nicole stepped off the bus—one of the boys pushed her into the girl in the bully group.

The girl pushed Nicole back into the boy and yelled, "Oh—so you want to fight! You think you are such hot stuff. What do you think of this?" as she punched Nicole in the face.

Nicole's little brother was just stepping off the bus as this all quickly happened. The bus driver ignored the fight, closed the door, and pulled down the street. The bully crowd walked home laughing as Nicole's brother helped his crying sister home.

As her middle-schoolers walked in the door, Nicole's mother was upset to hear crying. Once she calmed her daughter, she called the school to talk to an assistant principal. The assistant principal informed Mom that since this happened off school property, there was nothing that he could do.

Mom knew the families of the bullies (they had caused problems in the neighborhood before), and was pretty sure that their parents would not take any action to discipline the kids, so she waited for her husband to come home from work to discuss pursuing legal action.

Discussion

1. Was the assistant principal correct? Discuss this issue.
2. Did the bus driver have any responsibility in this situation?
3. How might a lack of action on the part of these school officials (leader and bus driver) have escalated this situation?
4. What is the current situation with regard to bullies in your schools?
5. What are some ways that schools deal with (or should deal with) bullying?

Further Discussion

In legal terms—discuss school jurisdiction with regard to bus stops.

LIP LICKING—AP HARASSMENT

Sexual harassment is an extremely sensitive subject in any work environment. It is especially frowned upon in the school setting. When a school employee feels harassed by a leader, it leads to a flood of emotions such as anger, surprise, intimidation, and fear. The following example is based on a true story, *Culture Shock* (Ostrovsky, D., 2005).

This article shares a story about a leader who continuously chose to sexually harass his teachers. One might think that most leaders would be in disbelief about such an event. Unfortunately, it happens far too often. In this case, it happened one too many times and is truly shocking.

Three elementary school teachers and one student teacher filed a sexual harassment lawsuit against the school's assistant principal. These educators alleged that Mr. Z., a vice principal at the school, engaged in stalking-type behavior and made inappropriate advances toward the women. They also accused the school's principal, Ms. P., of ignoring their reports. It seemed to them that Mr. Z. had been rewarded with a better position in Central Office following their reports (Ostrovsky, D., 2005).

While Mr. Z. was vice-principal, several allegations were made accusing him of inappropriate touching, suggestive comments, and sticking his tongue out in a sexually suggestive manner to a number of victims. On one occasion, Mr. Z., an African-American, told a teacher that he had "a chocolate bar" if she needed it. When a student teacher was called to his office regarding the dress code, Mr. Z. motioned to her suggestively (Ostrovsky, D., 2005).

Another teacher reported that he attempted to grope her on several occasions, and that he touched her back in front of students. He also made a reference to sex in front of the student teacher. Mr. Z. also asked one of the teachers to kiss him, and told her that he would have never married his wife if he had met her first. The educators felt that he was watching them and they felt stalked (Ostrovsky, D., 2005).

Court documents revealed that when the teachers confronted Ms. P. with the allegations, she surmised that perhaps Mr. Z. behaved in that manner because of his ethnicity, saying his behavior may be part of his culture. She also mentioned that he acted this way because he had worked in a high school. Ms. P. also later told one teacher that she was fabricating the whole story and acted as if nothing was wrong. She did not follow up to check on the allegations further (Ostrovsky, D., 2005).

The school division had an anti-harassment policy, which the school board attorney pointed out was followed meticulously. The attorney suggested that the lawsuit only contained allegations, and that there are two sides to every story.

Although the principal assured faculty that she would report the actions, she also advised teachers not to talk to lawyers. The teachers felt that the principal then began treating them differently following their reports (Ostrovsky, D., 2005).

Even after the school year ended, Mr. Z. called the student teacher on her cell phone and told her he wanted to get together with her and would "come and find her" if she did not call him back (Ostrovsky, D., 2005).

Ultimately, Mr. Z. was transferred to a more powerful position, and was in essence promoted.

The teachers finally got their own attorney, as the school division had failed to stop the harassment and reprimand the accused, and didn't even follow its own anti-harassment policy. The Equal Employment Opportunity Commission granted right-to-sue letters to the teachers, and they banned together and filed a civil suit against the principal, assistant principal, assistant superintendent, and superintendent of their school division (Ostrovsky, D., 2005).

Discussion

1. What would you have done differently if you were the principal dealing with this situation?
2. Should some individuals receive different consequences because of their cultural diversity? Explain.
3. Did the accusers in this article handle the situation appropriately? Explain
4. Did the Board of Education handle the situation appropriately? Explain.
5. How might the outcome be different if the principal had a conference with the AP when the allegations first began?

TO PAINT OR NOT TO PAINT

Schools are microcosms of society, and school leaders often find themselves dealing with social issues that come to the surface through changing times. Such issues as cell phone use and iPods in class were not issues that our teachers and leaders had to deal with even ten or fifteen years ago. In the last couple of years, body paint at school games has also become one of these modern issues.

Pilot-online, October 8, 2008 (pilotonline.com) reported that Grassfield High School students were told not to wear body paint to football games. A year earlier two girls in Florida were kicked out of a football game when they came to the game wearing bikini tops under body paint (Fox News, Oct. 2007). The girls questioned the outcome, as boys who had worn the body paint were not asked to leave games—but the girls had been told they were violating the dress-code.

An athletic association in North Carolina (WSOCTV.com Sept. 2007) banned body paint at games but allowed small face paintings. Ohio officials (Haroldtribune.com Oct. 2007) allow body-painting at outdoor games but not indoors. To paint or not to paint (bodies) seems to be an unresolved issue across the United States for school leaders.

For some time, teens across the country have been showing school spirit at football games, in similar fashion to those who attend professional football games, by wearing team apparel and head gear, waving banners, and—more recently—painting their bodies with team colors. Many teens and parents consider this an appropriate way for students to express school spirit. Some school officials, in response to those who violate the dress-code by removing shirts or wearing bikini tops in order to have more skin to paint, are opting for the preemptive tactic of banning body-painting at games.

Although some adults consider body-painting disruptive and inappropriate, others think it is an acceptable way to express school spirit and think that banning this ritual is taking away the students' right to free expression.

In the past year or two, body paint has become a more prevalent issue of controversy in schools across the country. There doesn't seem to be one solution (states, individual districts and individual schools are dealing with this in various ways), and school boards are finding this issue on their agenda more frequently. How should leaders deal with modern issues? Are issues ever escalated by taking an extreme measure when there may have been other options?

Discussion

1. What are the key issues for both students and school officials in the body-painting controversy?

2. Is body paint at football games an issue of free speech? Explain.
3. Can you think of any existing school policy that might cover this situation?
4. How should school officials approach this situation?
5. How might school officials work together with students, parents, and the community to solve this problem?

Further Discussion

Are there any First Amendment issues with regard to body paint? Are there any body-painting court cases?

DISAPPEARING STUDENT

Mr. Musalman (Mr. M.) was a new teacher. After his retirement from the military three years earlier, he had decided to go back to school, get his teaching license, and start his second career as a teacher. When he interviewed for the special education position at Liberty Middle School, the principal was impressed with his knowledge and life experience. The principal also was pleased to have another male role-model at this level.

The year started with the usual new teacher issues, as Mr. M. found his way around the building (he found his classroom—a portable located at the back of building), got to know other teachers, and worked his way through curriculum guides and handbooks. Being a male teacher with students in the 12–14 age range had its advantages, and Mr. M. had very few problems with discipline in his classes. There was one student (a sixth grade boy who was included for part of the day in Mr. M.'s class), Andy, who had a hard time sitting still and did not seem to pay attention.

Mr. M. opened his class one day by reading aloud from *A Bridge to Terabithia.* He explained to the class that they would be starting each day by taking turns reading aloud from the book. Andy looked down at the floor and started shuffling his feet when he heard that students would be taking turns reading aloud.

A few days later—Andy was asked to take his turn reading to the class. He told Mr. M. that he didn't feel like reading. Mr. M. insisted that everyone was going to take a turn and tried to hand the book to Andy. At that point, Andy slapped at the book and sent it flying across the room.

Mr. M. raised his voice and told Andy that his behavior was not appropriate. He asked Andy to step outside and wait for him there. Andy slammed the door of the portable as he left.

Mr. M. glanced out the window and saw Andy pacing back and forth outside the door. He handed the book to the next student designated to read and stood at the front of the class as the next chapter was read. After the read aloud was complete, Mr. M. referred the students to their independent work on the board and stepped outside to deal with Andy.

When he exited the portable, he was surprised to see that Andy was not waiting for him. He looked around the portable and called Andy's name—but he could not find Andy. This made him uncomfortable, but his first thought was that it was a little chilly and that Andy had most likely stepped inside the building. Mr. M. walked back into the classroom, wrote a quick note explaining the situation to the assistant principal, sent the note via student messenger to the main office, and continued teaching his class.

When Mr. M. went to the office during the lunch break, he was told that the assistant principal was in his office with Andy and Andy's mother.

He was asked to join them for the conference. As Mr. M. entered the office, he could tell that Andy's mother was very upset. She turned and hostilely asked, "Have you lost your mind? First, you insist that my dyslexic son read aloud to his class, and when he refused, you kick him out of the class. What kind of a teacher are you?"

As it turned out, Andy, a special education student included in Mr. M.'s class, had walked home instead of waiting for Mr. M. as he had been instructed.

Discussion

1. What training (school law, special education, school procedure, etc) should leadership have provided for this new teacher?
2. A quick Internet search reveals numerous stories of students left unattended in classrooms, on school buses, etc. This teen got home safely. What might have happened, and what responsibilities do school leaders, teachers, and bus drivers have in such situations?
3. How might this teacher have handled the situation differently?
4. What procedures should be in place with regard to classes held in portables to help keep our students and teachers safe?
5. What changes do you think need to be made in "safe schools" plans in light of our changing times?

I'M GOING TO CUT THE BABY OUT OF YOUR BELLY

The Learning Center (LC) at Patton Middle School was an active component of the school. Students assigned to classes in LC were usually there because they had an Individualized Education Program (IEP). The center was designed to allow teachers to team teach most of the time in an effort to meet individual needs.

There was one zone that was sectioned off intentionally to offer an area where teachers might work in small groups, or to allow students who needed time to cool down and think a more private space. Sometimes this area was used to isolate problem behaviors and allow other students to continue their work. The center had a team of teachers who each specialized in one special education area or another. Some taught learning disabilities and academic issues while others specialized in supporting students with behavior or emotional issues.

Ms. Rand specialized in behavior issues. She had only been teaching for four years, was young, and had just gotten married the year before. She was a good teacher, and the students and faculty all liked her. So when she told them in the fall that she was going to have a baby in early May, everyone was excited.

The LC was in the basement, and when everyone noticed that it was getting more difficult for her to go up and down the stairs with a heavy book bag that spring, there always seemed to be a student standing by to help her carry the bag up or down the stairs when she needed it. The students loved to volunteer their help and she was appreciative of such thoughtfulness from middle school students.

Ms. Johnson looked in on Ms. Rand one afternoon, and noticed that she was pale and looked uncomfortable. As she entered the room, she observed one student sitting in the back with a smirk on his face and his arms crossed over his chest. He seemed to be staring at Ms. Rand and not doing his work. Ms. Johnson approached Ms. Rand and asked her if everything was okay. Ms. Rand shook her head "no" and looked as if she was close to tears.

She got up and stepped out of the room. She turned sideways in an effort to keep one eye on the student as she whispered to Ms. Johnson. Ms. Rand said, "He" (as she nodded at the student) "threatened to cut the baby out of my belly." Ms Johnson was shocked.

She looked at Ms. Rand and questioned, "Are you telling me that the student in the back of your room threatened to cut the baby out of your belly?" Ms. Rand looked very upset by now and was very near tears. Ms Johnson asked further, "Why is he sitting there? Why didn't you send him out and get someone in here with you?"

Ms. Rand explained, "I did send him out. He made the comment during the last class and he went upstairs with another student to the office. The assistant principal talked to him and brought him back to class. He told me that the student needed to sit in my class until his parents get here to pick him up. He is having trouble getting in touch with the student's parents."

Ms. Johnson was shocked and very upset. As she quickly walked to the assistant principal's office, she thought there must be some kind of error or horrible misunderstanding. She was so upset that she walked right into the office. As she entered, the assistant principal looked up from his desk. He greeted her, smiled, and asked her to have a seat. Ms. Johnson remained standing and asked, "Why is the student who threatened Ms. Rand sitting in the room with her?"

The assistant principal explained that he had chatted with the young man and felt quite sure that he didn't mean what he said. He further explained that he hadn't been able to contact the parents to come and get him, so the student needed to be supervised by a behavior specialist (Ms. Rand) because of his IEP until his parents came to get him.

Ms. Johnson could not believe what she was hearing and very plainly told the assistant principal that she was very upset. She further explained that if he was wrong and anything happened to Ms. Rand, she would be the first to explain the situation to the police. At that point, she turned and left the office.

As she left, she also stated that she would be teaming with Ms. Rand for the rest of the day and that they would be holding their classes together so that Ms. Rand was not left alone with the offending student. Five minutes later, the assistant principal walked into Ms. Rand's room and took the student back to the office with him to wait for the parents. He did not speak to or give eye contact to Ms. Johnson for the remainder of the school year.

Discussion

1. Should a student with an identified Behavior/Emotional Disability be treated differently than other students because he has an IEP? Explain.
2. What options did this assistant principal have, and did he choose the correct option?
3. What might he have done? What would you have done?
4. What kind of trouble could Ms. Johnson have gotten in for walking in and talking to the assistant principal as she did?
5. What might Ms. Rand have done to avoid the situation in the first place?

Further Discussion

This student threatened bodily injury to the teacher. Discuss how this could have been a criminal law issue. This principal misinterpreted parameters of an IEP and failed to protect the teacher and other students. Do school leaders know enough about the law? Discuss teacher/leader preparation in this regard.

MOVE YOUR HAWK, MO!

Our First Amendment rights allow us freedom of expression, but where are the lines drawn? Specifically, the First Amendment of the Constitution states that "congress shall make no law respecting an establishment of religion, or prohibiting the free exercise thereof; or abridging the freedom of speech or of the press; or the right of the people peaceably to assemble, and to petition the Government for a redress of grievances" (pg. 5 - Russo, 2006).

It was a bright and sunny Monday morning. The birds were singing, the buses were on time, and the halls were buzzing with stories of the past weekend. In short, it was a great start to a wonderful, upcoming week.

As the day began, the principal noticed something blue, green, and tall-looking branching over the students' heads as a group came down the hall. As he focused on the color display he could see that it was someone's hair—a MOHAWK! Crayola colored and bright blue/green it was standing at attention.

The offending high school freshman turned a corner on his way to class. "Not so fast," called the principal, "Come to my office so we can talk." The student was a very respectful type, and had never been in any kind of trouble, so he abided by the principal's request.

Once in the office, the principal commenced a lecture about the youngster's hair and the inappropriateness of the style. "You cannot wear your hair in a Mohawk, and you *certainly* cannot color your hair! It's a distraction for other students and disrupts the learning environment," fumed the principal. The principal decided to punish the boy's "disruption." "You'll be suspended for two days and will serve your time in In-School Suspension (ISS). Now, I need to call your parents."

The student sat quietly while his father was called and notified of the incident. Within what seemed minutes, the student's father was racing down the hallway to loudly talk to the principal about his actions. The principal explained the dress code policy to the father and held firm on his choice of punishment. The father was not pleased and appealed the decision to Student Leadership.

In the end, the student was not required to serve ISS and there was nothing recorded in his school discipline record. He continued to wear his hair in a Mohawk fashion, and was sure to change the color from time to time, depending on the holidays or school events that took place.

Months later, the saga continues . . . The student was, again, in the hall with his hair.

The head of security for the school, an older gentleman of about sixty-five, really disliked this student's Mohawk. He would constantly come back to the assistant principal's office to complain about the student's hair and demand that something be done. The assistant principal (AP) repeatedly explained that nothing could be done. She explained that she had already talked to the student on several occasions and actually had a pretty good relationship with him.

In fact, the AP had talked to the student on several occasions and had a friendly relationship with him. She would ask to touch his hair to make sure that he did not put egg whites or glue in it that would make the hair hard (i.e., a weapon or safety issue). His hair, while extremely tall, was quite soft and was not dangerous.

Additionally, the assistant principal convinced the student to sit in the back of the classroom so he would not block other students' view of the chalkboard or overhead projector. After chatting with the student, she would always send him back to class as quickly as possible.

Near the end of the school year, the boy was sent *back* to the office again with a complaint about his hair!!! Another assistant principal, ready to retire, was talking to the head security guard in the hallway when the referenced student walked by. "Please go to the office and wait for me," requested the assistant principal.

The student did as he was told, and took his usual seat in the main office. The male AP then came to the female AP and asked that she "take care" of the situation, since she had dealt with the student in the past. She told him that she could not do anything, and explained that she had numerous conversations with the student about his hair.

She continued to explain that he sat in the back of the room so that he did not block others' view of instruction, he did not put any contents into his hair that would make it a safety hazard, and that she felt the adults were harassing the student!

The male AP, not happy with this response, told her to take care of it. She retorted back, "YOU take care of it!" As unprofessional as this was, it did happen. These two vice-principals had a friendly relationship prior to this incident. The principal overheard the fussing in the hall and was not happy. He put both APs in their place and then told the female AP to "take care of it."

Frustrated and ready to snap, she brought the student back to her office AGAIN. "Do you have any egg whites in your hair? Did you put any glue in your hair? Let me feel. Where are you sitting in each of your classes? Okay, go back to class." The incident was over, at least for the time being.

Discussion

1. Did the principal have a right, according to the First Amendment, to single out the student for his hair? Explain.

2. Could the situation have been handled differently so as not to cause a conflict between the school and the parent? How?
3. If the First Amendment is freedom of student expression, are students, then, allowed to express themselves by using foul language? How is this different from a hair or dress incident?
4. Did the APs handle the situation correctly? If not, why?
5. Did anyone fail to ask any pertinent questions that are necessary for this case?

Editorial Note from Dr. Willett for Further Discussion

"The Federal Circuit Courts of Appeal are divided in respect to restrictions on student hair, beyond safety and health issues. In those circuits that limit restrictions on student hair, they view unusual hair as a distraction rather than a disruption."—Dr. Willett

Discuss whether the issues of distraction and disruption in schools are the same.

BLANK ARM BANDS

Tinker v. Des Moines Independent Community School District (1969)

In 1969, *Tinker v. Des Moines Independent Community School District* addressed student rights at school for the first time. This has been one of the most significant cases in determining students' rights to expression at school. History documents a group of friends in 1965 who decided to wear black armbands to school in protest of the Vietnam War. School officials prohibited students from wearing the armbands and suspended them after they refused to remove them. School official found it necessary to suspend the students, as they wanted to "prevent the disturbance of school activities." (Street Law, 2000 Retrieved March 5, 2009).

In the United States, a country that values individual freedoms, it is important for any given school board to balance the need to maintain order and discipline with the rights of students. School authorities are charged with maintaining order and keeping students safe. To accomplish this, school authorities are allowed to take preventive or corrective measures in case of disruption. However, school authorities may not prohibit expression solely on the grounds that they do not agree with the students' viewpoint. "School officials could censor only when they could show that the expression would disrupt the school environment or invade the rights of other students" (Education Freedom, n.d.—Retrieved March 5, 2009).

After going all the way to the Supreme Court, it was determined that students and teachers have freedom of expression and speech in schools via the Constitution *(Russo, 2006, p. 839),* consequently asserting that these rights have to be respected (Education Freedom, n.d.—Retrieved March 5, 2009). This idea became the guiding principle for students' right to free expression. This ruling is often referred to as the "Tinker Test."

Under *Tinker,* "schools can regulate student speech whenever the school can show that the speech would be disruptive, or would interfere with the rights of other students" (Duffy, 2003). Tinker sets the scene to demand that schools cannot just make unilateral decisions to regulate student expression without justification (Russo, 2006). Ultimately, most courts understand that schools need varying levels of control depending on individual settings. But—in the end all must respect the rights of students to freedom of expression providing it does not disrupt learning.

Students have freedom with regard to their choice of dress as long as it does not disrupt the school. However, since 1968, students may not express themselves if they cause disruption or invade the rights of others (Russo, 2006).

The Supreme Court, in essence, ruled in favor of students saying that their actions did not violate constitutionally protected symbolic speech. Additionally, the Supreme Court's decision in Tinker v. Des Moines allowed students to express themselves freely in school if the expression was not in conflict with normal school operations. This case gave the rights of expression to students in multiple forums at their public educational institutions and continues to be looked upon as the cornerstone case in student expression rights.

Discussion

1. If students are allowed freedom of expression, does this carry over to using profanity as a form of expression? Explain.
2. If students, today, were to wear armbands in support or violation of a law or event, do you think the situation would be handled the same way? Explain.
3. What precedence has been set since Tinker v. Des Moines?

Editorial Note from Dr. Willett for Further Discussion

Compare Tinker with *Hill v. Lewis,* 323 F. Supp. (1991). In this later decision, the principal of Fayetteville High School in North Carolina refused to allow the wearing of black arm bands to protest continued involvement in Vietnam. The Federal District Court upheld the principal based on his decision that there would be a disruption, since large numbers of his students had fathers and other family in Vietnam. Pope Air force Base is in Fayetteville and was their departure point.

Discuss the two cases and compare/contrast key factors.

THE RIGHT TO PLAY

Leadership in schools goes beyond leadership from an administrative level. One often thinks of school leaders only as those from central office or the main office. Teacher and student leaders impact schools as models as much or more than those in designated leader positions. Students are always watching even those coaching extra-curricular activities. The following is taken from *The Hampton Roads Daily Press* February 20, 2008.

Tory Smart, a school band director, was arrested following a football game in 2008. Police found it necessary to shut down a Battle of the Bands due to fights that broke out in the stadium (Daily Press, 2008). Officers testified that Smart continued to direct the band while ignoring their requests for him to have the band stop playing, and Smart told the band not to listen to officers.

Smart's lawyer stated that the band had a First Amendment right to play. The case was dismissed as the judge said that he could not prove Mr. Smart's intent to obstruct justice. The judge did, however, strongly reprimand Mr. Smart's actions.

Discussion

1. What does the First Amendment state?
2. How does the First Amendment relate to this story?
3. Was Mr. Smart entitled to support his bands' First Amendment rights?
4. Beyond the First Amendment, what kind of a role model was Mr. Smart?
5. How do you think Mr. Smart's administrator should handle this situation?

Further Discussion

Discuss obstruction of justice. Although the judge decided this was not an obstruction of justice, how close did it come? If people were injured, might they have a right to sue band/school for damages incurred, as the band was not supporting law?

Chapter 4

An Expert Responds—Leading to Avoid Lawsuits and Hot Topics in Special Education Law

Willett Hall at Longwood University was named after Dr. Henry I. Willett, Jr. who was the president of the university from 1967–1981(Longwood, 2005). Dr. Willett also has spent over twenty years teaching at The George Washington University and continues to provide expertise as Professor Emeritus. Schools all over Virginia have been impacted as a result of Dr. Willett's consultation. This principled man is respected for his knowledge of leadership and savvy with regard to education and the law. His former students are impacted not only by his knowledge and skill, but also by his personable and supportive demeanor. Dr. Willett shares his "good sense" with teachers and leaders below.

DR. WILLETT'S COMMENTARY

Today's educator is well aware of a move in our society, the attempt to resolve many disagreements through litigation. It has become the norm for educational leaders to be threatened by parents, students, faculty, venders, or others with the words, "I'm going to sue." Fortunately, the bark is worse than the bite, and only a small percentage of these threats actually result in a courtroom drama.

The burden upon the educator remains, however. Regardless of whether a court action actually occurs, time and energy must be expended. In bringing these issues to closure, educators have to turn to preventive law. The practice of preventive law is designed to avoid litigation through anticipation and identification of potential legal pitfalls.

In the preceding pages, we have presented a number of potential legal issues in story form. A comprehensive listing of such issues is constantly changing, running the gamut from our old friend negligence to the new boy on the block, cyber-bullying.

Preventive law requires that faculty and staff receive updates dealing with changes in Federal and State law as well as with recent court decisions. There also should be a focus on policy at the district and school level. In order to be effective, policy should be understood and enforceable.

The thrust of any preventive law program is an emphasis on exercising good judgment and common sense. A review of the previous, noted stories reveals a lack of such.

An understanding and practice of preventive law should be coupled with the use of good judgment. If this is done, there is no reason to fear a judicial process that historically has recognized and supported sound educational leadership.

Finally, a preventive law program should be designed to inform, not frighten. We know, for example, that inaction can be just as deadly as wrongful action. The good news is that educators prevail about 75 percent of the time in litigation brought against them. For special education, the figure is closer to 55 percent.

In order to assist the implementation of preventive law a suggested outline has been provided for staff development purposes. Revisited annually, this outline has been used with over 800 faculty and staff groups (see Appendix A).

How the outline is used can be illustrated by the following brief review of the topic of sexual harassment. It is item (F) on the outline. Sexual harassment is a violation of Federal law. Adult to adult harassment falls under Title VI of the 1964 Civil Rights Act. Adult to student and student to student are covered under Title IX of the 1972 Civil Rights Act.

Generally, sexual harassment litigation involves suing both the alleged perpetrator and their supervisor or employer. The standard of proof against the supervisor is different for the two civil rights acts. Under Title VI, the supervisor "knew" or "should have known" of the harassment. Under Title IX, the supervisor must have had knowledge of the act.

Sexual harassment exists in two forms: a hostile environment and quid pro quo. Hostile environments can exist in multiple forms but frequently involve off color language and suggestive comments. Quid pro quo comes from the Latin "this for that." It contains an offer that if you will do this for me, I'll do that for you. An example would be a benefit to the employee in exchange for sexual favors.

In order to rise to the level of sexual harassment, the action must be severe, persistent, or pervasive. In September of 1996, a six-year-old Lexington, NC male student kissed a female classmate on her cheek. The school district punished the little boy, and received a very negative public reaction. It has since been determined that his action did not meet any of the criteria noted above.

There are going to be situations that are not always clear cut. The individual being harassed has an obligation to warn the harasser that their language and conduct is not welcome.

What can the school district do to avoid sexual harassment litigation?

1. Have a firm policy in place;
2. Train faculty and staff as to harassment issues; and
3. Investigate all charges of harassment on a good faith basis, documenting all findings.

The number of sexual harassment cases has actually declined in recent years, due largely to the steps noted above.

On the other hand, alertness and good judgment remain very important. Lest we think that this issue has gone away, the United States Supreme Court will hear a sexual harassment case involving a third grade boy and kindergarten girl in the Fall of 2008.

This brief discussion of sexual harassment serves as a model for covering other preventive law topics. Knowledge of potential problem areas precedes avoidance of litigation. Dr. Henry Willett, December 2008.

HOT TOPICS IN SPECIAL EDUCATION LAW

A survey of professionals, the Internet, and periodicals revealed the following repeated topics of interest with regard to the more specific area of special education and the law (Jewell, 2005). As Dr. Willett notes, "A recent Supreme Court decision placed the burden of proof on the party initiating the legal action. The greatest area of litigation centers on the services to be provided under the IEP."

Though the IEP (Individualized Education Program) presents the greatest area of litigation, special education law is a particularly complicated arena as reflected in the list of hot topics below. This list is by no means exhaustive, but offers some topics for further investigation and discussion. These topics might also provide a guideline for teacher/leader training or workshops.

Hot Topics in Special Education

NCLB

No Child Left Behind (NCLB) was passed in 2002 providing goals and guidelines intended to increase reading and math proficiency for all children.

The accountability of NCLB is considered by some to be at odds with the individualization mandated in the Individuals with Disabilities Education Act (IDEA), 1997, and most recently the Individuals with Disabilities Education Improvement Act (IDEIA- still generally referred to as IDEA), 2004 (Jewell, 2005).

The U.S. Department of Education Office of Special Education discusses alignment of IDEA with NCLB on its website (U.S. Department of Education, 2007). Topics such as definitions, funding, teacher qualifications, performance goals and indicators, assessments, and eligibility are discussed. Investigating this document and others at the CEC website provides interesting information to further discussion on these topics.

- Is NCLB (2002) at odds with the provisions of IDEA? Is one individual oriented while the other is group oriented? Do they support one another or address different groups?
- Or—did IDEA leave some behind, too? Are they more aligned to set higher standards for all?
- NCLB makes all more accountable and allows flexibility for states and districts. How does this translate to special education students?
- NCLB puts emphasis on "scientifically based" issues and provides options for parents. How does this translate to special education students?
- NCLB requires schools to report results and puts an emphasis on reading competence. How does this translate to special education students?
- Upcoming Court Case—State of Connecticut (CT) against U.S. Department of Education (USDOE)—CT asking for more funds and claiming USDOE exceeded authority. Another case out of U.S. 5th Circuit Court of Appeal upcoming. What impact might this have on special education programs?

Stimulus Funds

The U.S. Department of Education reports that more than $100 billion has been dedicated to education through the American Recovery and Reinvestment Act of 2009. Exact guidelines for how these funds will be disseminated and what they will be used for is currently being determined. Leaders would be wise to remain updated with regard to stimulus funding available for education. Some of this funding will be available for special education, and the CEC provides information about this funding at www.cec.sped.org (search Stimulus Funds). Some of the funds are being used to save and create teacher jobs during this time of economic stress. Other portions are being released to governors for discretionary use in individual states. Another portion has been earmarked for Title 1 and IDEA. The U.S. Department of Education is a great source for updated information regarding stimulus funding for education.

Of course—even funding for education can be controversial. Some possible topics of discussion include –

- For what are these funds allocated?
- Who might benefit from these funds?
- Are there funds available to K-12 in general and Special Education specifically?

Assessment & Testing

The accountability required by NCLB resulted in states and districts taking a closer look at their assessment and testing procedures. Several questions have been asked regarding the resulting tests and whether they truly meet the needs of all students.

- Do high stakes standardized tests best meet the needs of special education students?
- Do these tests violate the IEP?
- Are there better, more comprehensive ways to assess student progress?

Discipline/Manifestation

IDEA provides regulations to guide procedures for discipline of students with disabilities. Schools are given authority to consider unique situations, to remove students who cause bodily injury or bring weapons, and to remove a child who violates the code of conduct; IDEA also provides standards for manifestation determinations (IDEA Regulations, 2004).

- What is a manifestation determination?
- Do teachers and leaders understand the ten day rule?
- Schools have an obligation to protect. Are they successful?
- Required Hearing -- What are the parameters of the required hearing?

Assistive Technology

The Assistive Technology (AT) Act of 1998 provides support for AT centers, protection and advocacy, and low interest loans and financing for purchase of technology. More information is provided at: http://www.fctd.info/resources/techlaws.php.

- Are all leaders/teachers aware of these supports?
- Title I & Title III—Public Law requires accessibility and closed captions—What does that mean to schools?

- Wrights Law—resource—Does Wrights Law benefit teachers and leaders, too, or do they just advocate for parents/students?

Inclusion/Least Restrictive Environment

Schools are required to educate disabled students in classes with non-disabled students to the maximum extent appropriate. To this end the National Association of School Psychologists calls for inclusive schools (Inclusion, 2008).

- Is inclusion the answer for all students?
- What is meant by continuum of services?
- What is considered when determining the least restrictive environment?

FAPE—Free and Appropriate Education

Students are entitled to a Free and Appropriate Education for students with disabilities. This provision protects students from exclusion under Section 504 of the Rehabilitation Act of 1973 (Free and Appropriate Education, 2004).

- What is meant by "free and appropriate" education?
- What can be done if a parent or teacher thinks that an inappropriate placement has been made?

FERPA—Family Education Rights and Privacy Act

Family Education Rights and Privacy Act protects the privacy of students. Parents have the right to inspect records and to have records corrected. Schools must also have written permission to disclose records, and these rights are transferred to the child at eighteen years of age (FERPA, 2008).

- To what rights are parents entitled?
- What steps should leaders and teachers take to make sure that compliance is maintained?

Educator Rights

Teachers and leaders are tasked with the care of children each school day. This is an immense responsibility. In addition to this responsibility, educators also have personal and professional rights (Teachers' Rights).

- We know that students have rights. Do educators have rights, too?

- Torts—Constitutional Torts—What are they and what do they have to do with education?
- Intentional Interference—What is meant by "intentional interference?"
- Negligence—What constitutes "negligence?"

Transition

Transition is the process that prepares students with disabilities for their post-secondary experiences. Students should also be actively involved in this process.

- Indicators 13 and 14—What are the components of Indicator 13 and 14?
- What role do students and their families play in these plans?
- Are the current transition plans that are done by school systems sufficiently meeting the needs of individual students?
- School systems are required to contact students post-graduation to evaluate status (working, in school, training, etc). Is this being done?
- Adult agencies/partnerships with schools—are they effective?

Social Skills

With the current emphasis on academic success in school, teachers report finding less time available to teach social skills. However—these skills are often key to students' success both academically and in life in general.

- Is there a curriculum that addresses social skills?
- How are social skills addressed in an era of academic rigor?
- Is there generalization of social skills lessons to real life?

Advocacy/Parents Rights/Mediation/Due Process

Parents are often confused and feel powerless when faced with the complicated special education process. More frequently, parents are taking advantage of parent advocates to guide them through the process or support them when they think they are not getting the best education for their student. Teachers and leaders should consider themselves advocates for the students, too. Understanding parental rights, mediation, and due process is key to providing the best services possible for all students.

- What are parental rights?
- Often advocates are seen as antagonistic. How do we handle antagonistic parent advocates?

The above list of discussion topics addresses several issues that can complicate the educational process for special needs students, even culminating in legal situations if they are not handled correctly.

Shelly Smith (Smith, 2005) additionally shares what she calls the 7 Deadliest Sins of Special Education in her book *IDEIA 2004: Individuals with Disabilities Education Improvement Act: A Parent Handbook for School Age Children with Learning Disabilities.* Smith discusses procedural violations, denial of services based on cost, program rigidity, giving in to parents while violating FAPE, principle vs. reason, burden of proof, and procrastination as additional issues to consider when providing services for the special needs students. Leaders need to be sure that each of these seven is also addressed appropriately.

Obviously, special education and the law is a very specific and complicated area that leaders must deal with as they lead schools. On-going leader and teacher training on the above topics is important if schools intend to provide the best programs for our students and avoid legal quagmires.

Chapter 5

Dr. W. George Selig's Ten Leadership Principles: *What Good Leaders Do*

We sincerely hope that our stories and commentary have resulted in a few chuckles, some thoughtful discussions, and a resolve to positively impact leadership in our schools and beyond. In an effort to wrap up this book on a positive note, we are sharing (Dr. W. George) *Selig's 10 Leadership Principles.* Some of you may be asking, "Who is Dr. W. George Selig?"

Dr. Selig led Regent University as provost for eleven years and is currently (2009) a Distinguished Chair and Professor in the School of Education at Regent University.

His background includes extensive and diverse experience in public school systems as a teacher and administrator. He was Director of Special Education in several communities in Massachusetts, and became a leader in the development of the regulations for special education both at the state and federal level, serving on state committees in Massachusetts, and was also a Washington fellow in the writing of policy papers for federal law 94–142 in the late 1970's (Regent University Web site).

Beyond his Alaskan male-type, tough-guy expertise, Dr. Selig is a man of integrity and humor. Most think of him as someone who will guide them in the right direction with honesty, good sense, a quiet spirit, and occasionally a portion of tough love. He is a great role model for leaders, so we hope our readers might glean a lesson or two from his principles.

His *10 Leadership Principles* were gained through years of experience and informed by his faith. They can be used in any setting. We have listed them below, and they are followed by further explanation that connects them to current literature as it informs us about leadership. We hope you find these helpful in your own setting. We present—*Selig's 10 Leadership Principles.*

SELIG'S 10 LEADERSHIP PRINCIPLES

John 21:16, "Again Jesus said, 'Simon son of John, do you truly love me?' He answered, 'Yes, Lord, you know that I love you.' Jesus said, 'Take care of my sheep.'"

1. Care for the people you work with. Don't be concerned only with what they do for you at work. Be concerned about them, their lives, and their families. How can you serve them?
2. Trust the people who work for you. To improve, they need training—not threats. Trust them and they will rise to the level of your trust.
3. Praise others. This does not detract from you. Give and it shall be given unto you.
4. Use your heart, as well as your head, when looking for solutions.
5. Have a sense of humor.
6. Look for the best way or God's way—not your way.
7. See things through the eyes of the people you work with.
8. Earn respect. A position is given; respect is earned.
9. Help the people that you work with to grow so that they can become all that God wants them to be.
10. Plant love in the people who work for you and they will plant love in others and you will be truly enriched.

Let's take a closer look at each principle as we discuss them individually, and link these concepts to current leadership literature.

Principle #1—Care for the people you work with. Don't be concerned only with what they do for you at work. Be concerned about them, their lives, and their families. How can you serve them?

Principle #1 addresses the need to care for colleagues through service to them. This perspective naturally leads us to the concept of Servant Leadership.

Michael McKinney (Leadership Now, 2009) discusses choosing service over self-interest in leadership as he discusses George Washington's devotion to public service. Good leaders, as Selig and McKinney point out, take on the role of caretaker, and prioritize the best interest of others through service.

Serving others results in selflessness that is not often found in leaders. Truly serving others is based in such care and concern that one is able to do what is really best for the other. Leaders too often go first to—"How will this impact the workplace?" rather then—"How does this impact the individual?"

Concern for the company and the decisions that are made for any organization may result in an immediate gain for the organization but are sometimes at the expense of the individual. One example might be of a leader who denies time off for a personal situation by stating, "We have too much work to get done for you to take time off right now." That immediate gain, man-hours to complete the work, may initially result in the task at hand being completed in a timely manner to the benefit of the organization. However, those gains may be short-sighted if that denial of time off in fact results in an emotionally injured employee.

In the end—an escalated personal situation or losing the employee's dedication can reduce day-to-day productivity. Thus, that initial decision did not really benefit the organization or the employee in the long run. Leaders really need to give more thought to serving their employees, as those very employees provide support for the organization resulting in stronger, happier people who do a better job.

When one thinks of Servant Leadership, the work of Robert Greenleaf (Greenleaf, 2008) comes to mind. Greenleaf describes Servant Leadership as a combination of a natural inclination to serve intermingled with choice (Greenleaf, 2008). Although being a servant leader may come more naturally for some, one can also make the choice to focus more on service as a component of leadership.

Servant leaders put others first. Too often in leadership, we find leaders who further their own ambition and reputation (or that of an organization) over serving those people who work in that organization. Leaders and aspiring leaders might benefit from the study of the work of such authors as Robert Greenleaf, Stephen Covey, Peter Senge, and Ken Blanchard with regard to leading through service, and the components of Servant Leadership.

Principle #2—Trust the people who work for you. To improve, they need training—not threats. Trust them and they will rise to the level of your trust.

Trust in the workplace starts by choosing carefully the people you surround yourself with in the first place. It is important to look first for people with character, great work ethic, and commitment. They need to be people who believe what they do is a way of life and not simply a job.

If you give people responsibility, you need to give them authority to go and do what you asked them to do. Once the vision and goals are clear, you only manage to the degree necessary to ensure that the person can be successful. Give the people you work with the latitude and freedom to make a few mistakes and let them know you are solidly behind them encouraging, consulting, and supporting. Your trust, through this support, provides the framework, and once they feel your trust and support they will begin to achieve.

The Institute for Educational Leadership (IEL) reported results from a survey which indicated that trust was essential to leadership. Trust seems to correspond with innovation, creativity, and reform (IELeadership, 2003). Fostering trust in schools should be a primary focus for educational leaders.

Principle #3—Praise others. This does not detract from you. Give and it shall be given unto you.

It is important to praise people for their successes and give them credit where credit is due. This praise does not detract from you as a leader. It only enhances loyalty and commitment. Leaders need to make sure that praise is an honest representation of appreciation for a job well done, or with a laudatory attitude. If praise is simply a manipulation technique, it destroys trust and loses any meaning. Byham (1992) stresses the importance of enhancing teacher self-esteem by regularly giving positive feedback through constructive comments regarding their work performance.

Kevin Eikenberry at *The Sideroad* (2007) suggests that leaders use the written word to present positive reinforcement. Notes, letters, and email can be reread for a more long-lasting effect.

There are numerous studies that indicate the importance of leaders using positive reinforcement. One study, *Analyzing the Leadership Behavior of School Principal (*Bulach, C. Boothe, D., & Pickett, W., 2006) found that human relations factors (including leaders providing positive reinforcement) were very important to successful leadership. Positive reinforcement, whether in the form of verbal, written, or tangible rewards, is an effective leadership tool when used appropriately.

Byham (1992) introduces the concept of Zapping (empowering as opposed to Sapping—taking power), or giving power to employees. Leaders who Zapp encourage meaningful work environments through teamwork, trust, praise, communication, flexible controls, challenges, and recognition, rather than providing no authority in an environment that lacks resources and novelty—which would allow little room for growth (Byham, 1992).

Principle #4—Use your heart, as well as your head, when looking for solutions.

A machine can be programmed to make an analytical decision, but what it can't do is factor in the human element. People have emotions, feelings, experiences, and special talent, along with needs, all of which are related.

As leaders make decisions, they need to consider those affective aspects because they may hold the key to success and long term prosperity. Educational leaders have been called to teach, nurture, and lead not only an organization, but also the people within it. True leadership requires you to think about the people, not just the dollar and cents. It also means that sometimes your heart will prevail over a purely cognitive decision. Leaders need to be open to allowing that to happen. Oftentimes the results are rewarded with increased commitment, loyalty, and trust, which is beneficial in the long term.

William C. Taylor (2008) suggests that people support causes they believe in and that leaders should appeal to both the heart and the head. Leaders are more effective if they use both their heads and their hearts as they make decisions and deal with people in organizations.

Nothing touches our hearts more than our families. Leaders can show heart by supporting employees as they balance family and work obligations. A study by the U. S. Department of Labor supports the importance of organizations supporting families. *The Role Of The Work Environment And Job Characteristics In Balancing Work And Family* (Berg, P., Appelbaum, E. & Kalleberg, A., 1999) concludes that high performing organizations support that balance of family and work obligations. Leaders need to consider using their hearts and well as their heads when making decisions, and this includes considering ways to support families in the workplace.

Principle #5—Have a sense of humor.

There are very few situations in which a little humor is not refreshing, tension breaking, and humanizing. Look for the humor, as there is something a little humorous in most every situation. Humor tends to build a togetherness and sense of community.

Humor also provides the relief valve that frees people up to be more creative. It takes away the tension that inhibits progress and free and open exchanges. Humor also contributes to good mental health. A win/win situation is created in organizations that provide tension-free environments, allow room for creativity, and promote good mental health through humor!

Perhaps Billy Graham says it best, "A keen sense of humor helps us to overlook the unbecoming, understand the unconventional, tolerate the unpleasant, overcome the unexpected, and outlast the unbearable" (Thinkexist.com)

Principle #6—Look for the best way or God's way—not your way.

For those of faith, going to God with plans leads to thinking about things in a more complete way and helps to take self out of the middle. Dr. Selig states, "I try to get away from what I want and get to what truly is best. I have to die to self a little bit."

For those leaders who are not informed by their faith, it is still a matter of selflessly leading to find the best way and not always trying to get their own way.

Really handing situations at work to God, for those of faith, allows leaders to be open and to think of other ways to proceed with an openness to the thoughts of others, and ultimately be able to make a more balanced decision. Faithful leaders need to be praying in order to admit their way may not be the best way, and that other ideas may have more merit.

Dr. Selig's faith informs his practice, and this concept can be expanded to speak to leadership issues that are pertinent to all leaders. It is important to take self out of the middle of decisions and to be open to the thoughts of others while making balanced decisions.

Principle #7—See things through the eyes of the people you work with.

Organizations are really about relationships. The climate, productivity, and loyalty present in an organization are directly related to the leader's ability to build relationships. An organization can be successful in the short run without good relationships, but long term a price is paid because there is no organizational resilience.

When down turns come or reaching down for that little extra crunch is required, relationships will carry you. Putting yourself in another person's shoes is key to relationships and to understanding issues from a different perspective. Being able to do this strengthens your relationships and encourages others because they truly know they have been heard.

Karen Dyer in *Relational Leadership* (2001) addresses issues of relational leadership. Dyer suggests that leaders need to gather feedback from all stakeholders in an effort to be sure that positive relationships are in place. Sustaining relationships, building teams, managing conflict and change, as well as confronting problems are important components that successful leaders develop in organizations (Dyer, 2001). It is important for leaders to be aware of the complicated nature of relational aspects of an organization, and to work to improve these characteristics.

Principle #8—Earn respect. A position is given; respect is earned.

Leaders are given respect because of their position. However, if they don't additionally have a commitment to earning respect through their behavior, commitment, and leadership abilities, they squander the opportunity to have respect that goes beyond simply the power of the position.

People will rally around a leader and give them (not just their position) support and commitment if they truly respect that leader. It is also important that leaders show respect in return. Without this reciprocal respect, only lip service exists, leaving the leader truly alone in his or her position.

Don Clark addresses the issue of earning and modeling respect in *Concepts of Leadership* (2008). Clark points out that leaders are being observed, and that modeling positive character traits, including respect, is an imperative component of good leadership (2008). Leaders need to be aware of what character traits are being observed by followers in order to gain respect that goes beyond the respect garnered by the position.

P*rinciple #9—Help the people you work with to grow so that they can become all that God wants them to be.*

Everyone has a destiny. Leaders have the responsibility to facilitate the growth and development of those who work for them in an effort to help them prepare to fulfill their destiny.

Sometimes people get opportunities, and these may be inside or outside your organization. It is important to celebrate these opportunities. Never begrudge an opportunity that may result in a better position, even if it may result in the organization losing a valuable person.

When people know you value them enough to celebrate their growth and promote them as excellent employees, they will give more and are more effective. God will always replace a winner with another winner when you have helped one to grow and move on.

Bruce Wilkinson addresses this issue of destiny in his book *The Dream Giver (*2003). Through an easily understood parable, Wilkinson points out that we are all given a dream, but that we often will fall short of accomplishing what we were meant to do as we work to overcome obstacles and conquer fears (Wilkinson, 2003). Thus it is important for leaders to maintain focus and tenacity as they accomplish their destiny.

Principle #10—Plant love in the people who work for you and they will plant love in others and you will be truly enriched.

Ultimately, leadership comes down to loving people and wanting the best for them. Good leadership creates tremendous relationships and trust, and calls people to become the best they can be. A leader who leads with love will be blessed with that love in return, and an organization will reflect love in its performance, policies, and commitment to one another.

Bruce Winston (2002) in *Be a Leader for God's Sake* points out that leaders need to expand the Golden Rule of *do unto others as you would have them do unto you* to the Platinum Rule to *do unto others as they would want you to do.* Winston (2002) expands this concept of love to be reflected in how the leader treats others. Leaders need to encourage others and treat them as intelligent, creative human beings. He goes on to point out that loving leaders also set high expectations, and in that regard are also often considered tough (Winston, 2002).

Leaders need to be sure that employees' gifts are aligned with their jobs, and should encourage growth. In rare cases—when an employee simply is not in alignment with the needs of the organization—the loving leader may also have to ask them to leave. Finally leading in love is not the sweet and syrupy type of love one might initially think of when discussing love, although it does consider the best interests of all.

In Conclusion—Dr. Selig shares the following thoughts. Leadership is not simply a job you to do to help your organization become successful. It is a way of life in the process of helping people become more Christ-like in their thoughts and actions. Your job is the vehicle that allows the added opportunity to share the joy and love of Jesus Christ in a way that provides the opportunity for growth. –Dr. Selig January 28, 2009

Dr. Selig's faith guides his leadership principles. As discussed above, Dr. Selig's principles are directly reflected in current leadership theory. All leaders, whether of faith or not, can learn from his universal principles as they consider leadership to be not only a job, but also an opportunity to help each employee grow.

Chapter 6

Summary and Conclusions: The Future an Invitation for More Stories

Modern schools are more complicated than ever before in history. New laws, savvy parents, and advances in technology all enhance our schools as they advance the education of our twenty-first century students while simultaneously complicating the role of the leader. Leaders need more extensive preparation in order to meet these challenges. Whether for teacher leaders, coaches, counselors, or administrators, on-going training that raises both professional awareness and skills is necessary to ensure that leaders make the right choices when under pressure and presented with sensitive situations.

Ultimately, tragic situations like the heatstroke death of a high school football player need to be avoided (Startribune.com, 2009). The avoidable horror of a young life being cut short is a prime example that shows why it is imperative for leaders to provide on-going training. In this heatstroke case, for the first time in history, a coach is being indicted on criminal charges. It is more important now than ever before to be sure that our leaders and teachers are as prepared as they can be to benefit and protect students in our schools.

Leaders need to be prepared to make the right decisions at all times. Hopefully, this book has provoked thought that will guide leaders as they continue their own professional growth and provide on-going training for faculty and staff. We hope that stories like these reduce the number of leadership bloopers and blunders! Further resources to support leadership growth can be found in Appendix B. At the end of the day, making the right decisions will benefit the students as excellence in education is achieved.

**We would like to hear your unbelievable stories. If you have a story that you would like to share (we always change the names to protect the guilty ☺ or the innocent), please contact Dr. Hope Jordan at Regent University (hopejor@regent.edu). Just put "Leadership Bloopers and Blunders" in the subject line, and we will contact you as soon as we can.

Appendix A

Dr. Willett's Outline Preventive Law and Education

I. Introduction

   A. Preventative law—prevention through anticipation, using good judgment

   B. Legal decision-making with an emphasis on policy

II. Improper Physical Contact—All forms of physical contact with students including corporal punishment (banned in over half the states), touching, and sexual misconduct

III. Reporting Child Abuse and Neglect

IV. Negligence and Adequacy of Supervision—Foresee-ability

   A. Criteria for negligence—both acts of negligence and failure to act

   B. Defenses & immunity

   C. Simple vs. gross negligence—willful misconduct, deliberate indifference, and reckless disregard

   D. Leaving students unattended

   E. Other high-risk situations—shops, labs, PE and athletics, field trips, recess, transportation, locker rooms, use of private vehicles

   F. Summary—are schools the guarantor or insurer of safety? Do the schools have a duty to protect?

V. Religion—Prayer and Other Observances, Curriculum—Applicability to Students, to Teachers. Pledge of Allegiance

VI. Safety and Discipline
   A. Safety vs. privacy and constitutional protections
   B. Due process and discipline, regular and special education
   C. Search and surveillance—avoid strip searches
   D. Student dress and expression—distraction vs. disruption.
   E. Bullying, hazing
   F. Sexual harassment—severe, persistent, pervasive
      1. Adult to adult, Title VI
      2. Adult to student, Title IX
      3. Student to student Title IX

VII. Academic and Related Issues—Who determines the curriculum, duty to follow, etc.
   A. Fairness and consistency—grading and other policies
   B. Requests to opt out
   C. Accountability and educational malpractice

VIII. Evolving and Emerging Issues—Technology—Cyber Bullying—Cell Phones, Teacher Expression, Affirmative Action, Single Sex Education, Off-Campus Jurisdiction, Suicidal Student, FERPA—Confidentiality

IX. Summary

X. Questions

Prepared by Dr. Henry I. Willett, Jr.
Virginia Beach, VA
mhwillett@cox.net

Appendix B

WEB RESOURCES

- EdGate Special Education and Gifted Center
  http://www.edgateteam.net/sped_gifted/hot_topicviolence.htm
  This interactive site invites reader participation. EdGate Special Education and Gifted Center site provides contemporary hot topic links that address current issues in education. This site includes information on violence and safety, assessment, assistive technology, character education, English as a second language, gender equity, home schooling, inclusion, school to work, and social skills.

- Leadership Qualities http://www.nsba.org/sbot/toolkit/LeadQual.html
  This link provides ten qualities that provide insight into whether a person has the propensity to lead. Some are born with the natural ability to lead. Others can learn to be better leaders. This site explores propensity to lead, character traits important to good leadership, and the skills needed to lead.

- The Lighter Side of Teaching
  http://teachers.net/gazette/JUN03/humor.html
  This site offers cartoons and stories intended to make you smile or break out in a belly laugh. Teaching is very stressful and too often we take ourselves too seriously. Sometimes we need to just stop for a laugh or a smile. Several reasons to laugh can be found at this site.

- Mistakes Educational Leaders Make
  http://eric.uoregon.edu/publications/digests/digest122.html

In alignment with our book, this article highlights leadership mistakes. The article takes a look at mistakes, interpersonal communication, leadership training, and closes with suggestions on how to avoid mistakes.

- Defining Workplace Harassment
  http://www.beyondbullying.co.nz/defining_workplace_harassment.htm
  This article discusses the process of defining workplace harassment and bullying from a global perspective. Suggestions for how to deal with workplace harassment are also provided.

- Tinker versus Des Moines
  http://www.bc.edu/bc_org/avp/cas/comm/free_speech/tinker.html
  This link provides the details for the Supreme Court Case of Tinker versus Des Moines when tackling the issue of First Amendment rights.

- Understanding the Crime of Forgery
  http://www.uslawbooks.com/books/forgery.htm
  The link provides basic law regarding forgery and further discusses how to prove and when to prosecute forgery.

- Wrightslaw http://www.wrightslaw.com/
  Wrightslaw provides a wealth of information regarding special education law, education law, and advocacy for students with disabilities. This resource offers access to books, articles, cases, and resources on topics that range from IDEA 2004 and special education law to advocacy.

BOOKS

- *The Art of School Leadership*
  Thomas Hoerr
  ASCD (2005)
  This book discusses the complicated issues of leadership. Hoerr suggests that successful leaders go beyond just analyzing data to also develop relationships and handling human issues. The book takes a comprehensive look at leadership.

- *The Learning Leader: How to Focus School Improvement for Better Results*
  Douglas Reeves
  ASCD (2006)

Douglas Reeves suggests that leaders look at more than test scores when designing school improvement plans. Reeves encourages leadership teams and reflective leaders in effective schools.

- *Jay McGraw's Life Strategies for Dealing with Bullies*
  Jay McGraw
  Simon & Schuster (2008)
  This book addresses the complicated issue of bullying. McGraw takes a look at bullying from the victim's, the bully's, and the by-stander's perspective and discusses how to deal with this situation.

- *Wrightslaw: Special Education Law*
  Peter and Pamela Wright
  Harbor House Law Press (2007)
  Wrightslaw includes information on Child's Right to a Free, Appropriate Public Education (FAPE); Individualized Education Programs (IEP); IEP Teams; Transition & Progress; Evaluations, Reevaluations, Consent & Independent Educational Evaluations; Eligibility & Placement Decisions; Least Restrictive Environment, Mainstreaming & Inclusion; Research Based Instruction; Discrepancy Formulas & Response to Intervention; Discipline, Suspensions & Expulsions; Safeguards, Mediation, Confidentiality, New Procedures; and Timelines for Due Process Hearings.

- *Contemporary Issues in Leadership* (sixth edition)
  Edited by William Rosenbach and Robert Taylor
  Westview Press (2006)
  This book is an anthology of essays that address issues of vision, values, culture, development, and outcomes. Current research and practical applications of leadership distinguishes this book from others.

- *Managing Leadership Stress*
  Vidula Bal
  Center for Creative Leadership (2008)
  Leadership can be very stressful whether in educational leadership or the business world. Stress can be detrimental to health. This book helps identify the signs of stress and suggests ways to deal with stress.

References

Berg, P., Appelbaum, E., and Kalleberg, A., (1999). The role of the work environment and job characteristics in balancing work and family. http://www.dol.gov/oasam/programs/history/herman/reports/futurework/conference/balance/bergappelbam.htm.

Bulach, C., Boothe, D., and Pickett, W. (2006). Analyzing the leadership behavior of school principals. http://www.westga.edu/~cbulach/sclimate/lsp.htm. Retrieved 1/16/08.

Byham, W.C. (1992). *Zapp! In education: How empowerment can improve the quality of instruction and student and teacher satisfaction.* New York: Ballantine Books.

Clark, D. (2008) Concepts of leadership. http://www.nwlink.com/~donclark/leader/leadcon.html.

Daily Press (2008). High school band director arrested. www.dailypress.com. Retrieved 12/28/08.

Duffy, S. (2003). Modified 'Tinker' Test applied to case involving grade school students. http://www.law.com/jsp/article.jsp?id=1050369425646. Retrieved 7/14/08.

Dyer, K. (2001). Relational leadership. School Adminstrator. http://www.aasa.org/publications/saarticledetail.cfm?ItemNumber=3224.

Eikenberry, Kevin. (2007). The sideroad. http://www.sideroad.com/Leadership/example-of-positive-reinforcement.html. Retrieved 4/15/09.

Education for Freedom. (n.d.) Lesson plans for teaching the First Amendment. http://www.freedomforum.org/packages/first/Curricula/EducationforFreedom/supportpages/L08-CaseSummaryTinker.htm. Retrieved 7/14/08.

Encyclopedia of Everyday Law. Teachers' rights. *http://www.enotes.com/everyday-law-encyclopedia/teachers-rights.* Retrieved 12/2/08.

Family Center on Technology and Disability. http://www.fctd.info/resources/techlaws.php.

FERPA Family Education Rights to Privacy Act. (2008). Ed.gov. http://www.ed.gov/policy/gen/guid/fpco/ferpa/index.html

Free and Appropriate Public Education for Students with Disabilities. (2007). Ed.gov. http://www.ed.gov/about/offices/list/ocr/docs/edlite-FAPE504.html.

Greenleaf Center for Servant Leadership. (2008). http://www.greenleaf.org/

Google — http://www.google.com/support/jobs/bin/static.py?page=benefits.html.

IDEA Regulations 2004 Building the Legacy. (2004). U. S. Department of Education (OSEP)— IDEA, Discipline. *idea.ed.gov/frontend_dev.php/object/fileDownload/model/Presentation/field/PresentationFile/primary_key/19.* Retrieved 1/6/09.

IELeadership. (January/February 2003). Institute for Institutional Leadership IELeadership Connections. eNewsletter V1, No. 3, Trust (Commentary). http://www.iel.org/news/newsletter/jan03.html#trust.

Inclusion, Least Restrictive Environment (LRE), Mainstreaming. (2008). Wrightslaw. http://www.wrightslaw.com/info/lre.index.htm. Retrieved 12/20/08.

Jewel, M. E. (2005). "No Child Left Behind" implications for special education students and students with limited English proficiency. *New Horizons for Learning.* http://www.newhorizons.org/spneeds/improvement/jewell.htm. Retrieved 2/21/09.

Leadership Now. (2009). http://www.leadershipnow.com/service.html.

Longwood Magazine. (2005). Winter celebrating leadershi. vol. 5, no. 2. http://www.longwood.edu/longwood/winter05/leadership.htm.

Ostrovsky, D. (2005). Berlin intermediate school teachers file harassment suit in U.S. http://findarticles.com/p/articles/mi_qn4183/is_20050823/ai_n14914016/print. Retrieved 3/3/08.

Russo, C. J. (2006). *Reutter's the law of public education* (6th ed.). New York: Foundation Press.

Russo, C. J. (2006). Reutter's the law of public education (6th ed). *Tinker v. Des Moines.* New York: Foundation Press.

Smith, S. (2005). *IDEA 2004: Individuals with disabilities education improvement act: A parent handbook for school age children with learning disabilities.* Author House: Bloomington, IN.

Startribune.com. Crockett tragedy heatstroke football player. http://www.startribune.com/lifestyle/health/38154204.html?elr=KArks7PYDiaK7DUvDE7aL_V_BD77:DiiUiacyKUnciaec8O7EyUr.

Street Law, Inc. and the Supreme Court Historical Society. (2000). *Tinker v. DesMoines* [1969]. http://www.landmarkcases.org/tinker/pdf/tinker_v_des_moines.pdf. Retrieved 3/6/09.

Taylor, William C. (2008). On leadership—less head, more heart. WashingtonPost.com. http://views.washingtonpost.com/leadership/panelists/2008/12/less-head-more-heart.html.

Thinkexist.com. http://thinkexist.com/quotation/a_keen_sense_of_humor_helps_us_to_overlook_the/157038.html. Retrieved 10/30/08.

Transition Ed.gov. http://www.ed.gov/about/offices/list/ocr/transition.html.

U.S. Department of Education. (2007). Alignment with No Child Left Behind Act. http://idea.ed.gov/explore/home. Retrieved 1/16/09.

Wilkinson, B. (2003). *The dream giver.* Sisters, OR: Multnomah Publishers, Inc.

Winston, B. (2002). Be a leader for God's sake. http://www.bealeaderforgodssake.org//Pilot Online http://hamptonroads.com/2008/10/bodypainting-games-banned-grassfield-high-school—body painting. Retrieved 2/8/09.

http://www.foxnews.com/story/0,2933,303037,00.html. Florida body paint. 10/17/07.

http://www.heraldtribune.com/article/20071019/NEWS/71019009. Ohio body painting. 10/07.

http://www.wsoctv.com/highschoolsports/14066595/detail.html. Charlotte, NC. 9/07.

10News.com. *http://www.10news.com/news/1515763/detail.html.*

10News.com. http://www.10news.com/news/1424826/detail.html.

About the Authors

Hope M. Jordan is a professor in the School of Education at Regent University where she directs special education teacher licensure and codirects leadership with special education emphasis. Her presentations, publications, teaching experiences, and consulting keep her on the cutting edge in the field of education.

Henry I. Willett is a former public school administrator and college president. He taught school law at multiple institutions and has given over eight hundred school law presentations to public and private schools.

W. George Selig is a longtime school leader with administrative experience across grade levels from K to 12 to postgraduate in a variety of settings from rural America to large cities. He has never lost his zeal for education and for the students it serves.

Andrea P. Beam is an assistant professor at Liberty University. She has experience in administration, special education, and elementary education.